Explore the Cape Flora

Written and illustrated by
Margo Branch

Photographs by George Branch

CAMBRIDGE
UNIVERSITY PRESS

PUBLISHED BY THE SYNDICATE OF THE UNIVERSITY OF CAMBRIDGE
The Pitt Building, Trumpington Street, Cambridge CB2 1RP, United Kingdom

CAMBRIDGE UNIVERSITY PRESS
The Edinburgh Building, Cambridge CB2 2RU, United Kingdom
40 West 20th Street. New York, NY 10011-4211, USA
10 Stamford Road, Oakleigh, Melbourne 3166, Australia
1 The Moorings, Portswood Ridge, Victoria and Alfred Waterfront,
Cape Town 8001, South Africa

Design and typesetting Angela Ashton

First published by Struik Publishers, Cape Town, 1987
First published by Cambridge University Press, 1999

Colour reproduction by Mega Pre-Press cc, Cape Town
Printed in South Africa by Paarl Printing (Pty) Ltd

Typeset in Concorde and Meta

ISBN 0 521 58553 8 paperback

Other titles in this series
Explore the Seashore of South Africa

Acknowledgements
This book has been a great joy to me as it encompasses many memorable outings and experiences with friends and family. My particular thanks to my husband George whose enthusiasm and wonderful photographs inspired me to tackle the book. Our children Bryony and Trevor have shared in the project and helped with essential computing assistance.
I have drawn heavily on the advice and research of botanists, zoologists and geologists from the University of Cape Town, the Bolus Herbarium and Kirstenbosch National Botanical Gardens. My particular thanks go to Dr Peter Goldblatt, Dr John Rourke, Dr John Rodgers, Anne Bean and Professor William Bond. With patience and encouragement, the late Bertie Jessop taught me the joys of watercolour painting. My thanks to Pieter Struik for his help during the first edition of the book and for permission to adapt the map on the Cape Floral Kingdom from 'Fynbos' by R Cowling and D Richardson.

Photographic acknowledgements
Scanning electron microscope photographs of pollens (page 33): Restio – P Linder; Brunia – A V Hall; China Flower – P A Bean. Lesser Double Collared Sunbird (back cover) Percy FitzPatrick Institute of African Ornithology, University of Cape Town.

All other photographs by G M Branch

Map of Cape Floral Kingdom – B A Branch

Contents

Introduction

In a narrow strip of land at the southern tip of Africa is a living treasure. This is the Cape Floral Kingdom. Nowhere else in the world are there so many different species of plants in such a small area. The scenery is spectacular and from the dramatic rugged mountains – of which Table Mountain is the most famous – one can survey the coastal plains, rocky headlands and golden beaches of both the Atlantic and the Indian Oceans. The living treasure is best viewed close up because the aromatic plants produce a fascinating array of colourful and unusual flowers that attract many birds, insects and other small creatures.

Tragically, this delicately balanced ecosystem is under threat from introduced species and human development, and some plants and animals have already become extinct. The region is being actively conserved with strict laws about picking flowers, the elimination of alien vegetation and the formation of many protected areas. The recently proclaimed Cape Peninsula National Park, which includes the mountain range from Table Mountain to Cape Point, protects a natural wonderland on the doorstep of Cape Town – the most visited area in South Africa and home to 3 million people.

The Cape Flora has found its way into gardens world-wide, but don't miss out on the thrill of discovering it in the wilds.

Come and explore.

The Cape Floral Kingdom

The Cape Floral Kingdom stretches from Nieuwoudtville in the west to Port Elizabeth in the east. It is a hot-spot of biodiversity with many more species per unit area than anywhere else in the world. A heath-like vegetation known as fynbos covers 80 per cent of the region. The rest of the flora is made up of renosterveld, succulent karoo vegetation and small patches of forest and thicket (see map on page 59).

Typical fynbos vegetation in Kirstenbosch gardens, patches of thicket and forest grow in the distance.

Fynbos (fine bush)

The characteristic plants of the fynbos are proteas, colourful ericas, hardy Cape reeds and plants known as geophytes that survive harsh conditions underground as bulbs. Fynbos grows in areas with more than 300 millimetres of rain, most of it falling in winter. It favours nutrient-poor soil, often has small leaves to reduce wilting during the dry summer, and is fire-adapted (see pages 12–20).

Renosterveld (rhinoceros veld)

Renosterveld is characterised by low-growing grey bushes known as renosterbos *Elytropappus rhinocerotis*. These were perhaps named after the rhinoceros that once roamed the area. Renosterveld occurs where there is moderate winter rainfall, between 250 and 600 millimetres per year, and fertile clay soil. This is the region most in demand for farm land and only 3 per cent of the original renosterveld has survived.

Left:
Over 95% of the renosterveld has been replaced by farmlands, leaving tiny strips of grey renosterveld in less accessible spots.

Right:
A spectacular spring display near Vanrynsdorp where renosterveld merges into succulent karoo vegetation.

Succulent karoo plants have fleshy leaves and occur in low rainfall areas.

Succulent karoo vegetation

Sparse, low-growing succulent karoo vegetation is found in dry areas with less than 250 millimetres of predominantly winter rain and where the soil is rich in nutrients. The karoo, from the khoekhoe word for 'dry', is the semi-desert region in the rain shadow north of the Cape Fold Belt Mountains and along the west coast approaching Namaqualand. It has the highest number of plant species for a semi-arid area anywhere in the world. The most common of its fleshy leafed plants are the vygies, with over 2 000 species (see pages 28 and 42).

things to do

Discover the climatic conditions of South Africa by following the weather reports on television. Cold fronts bring winter rainfall to the Western Cape at roughly 7-day intervals.

Subtropical thickets

Dense thickets of bush or low forest occur along rivers, dunes and on termite mounds (known as heuweltjies). Thickets thrive in nutrient rich soils with a rainfall of between 300 and 800 millimetres and where there is little danger of fire. The bushes in these thickets are not confined to the Cape and also occur along the east coast. Many of them have fleshy fruits.

did you know?

There are an astounding 8 600 different plant species in the Cape Floral Kingdom, even although it covers only 90 000 square kilometres – a mere 0.04% of the world's surface. Of these, 5 800 are endemic to the region which means they occur naturally nowhere else in the world. Many of the species are rare and endangered.

Afromontane forest

Small pockets of cool temperate forest occur in areas of high year-round rainfall of over 800 millimetres. The most important trees are the magnificent yellowwoods. Knysna forest in the southern Cape is the only extensive forest in the region.

Enormous yellowwoods – the 'big' trees in the Knysna Forest.

Table Mountain – symbol of the Cape

Table Mountain dominates the lives of Cape Town's 3 million inhabitants. It towers majestically over the city, influencing weather patterns, creating shelter from the ferocious winds and lifting the spirits of daily commuters with the beauty of its misty tablecloth and sunlit cliffs. The Cape Peninsula National Park stretching from Table Mountain to Cape Point provides an opportunity for all to experience the wonders of the Cape Floral Kingdom.

Rare **Table Mountain ghost frog** clings to stones in fast-flowing streams

did you know?

The Cape Peninsula was once an island cut off from the rest of Africa by the sea. One frog, 111 invertebrates and 90 plants are endemic to the Cape Peninsula.

A bird's-eye view of the Cape Peninsula

Rocky foundations

The Cape Peninsula, with its hard rocks, has endured the relentless forces of waves, rain and wind. Table Mountain has weathered down from a height of 3 000 to 1 050 metres but the Cape Flats have been flattened.

Youngest rocks – Table Mountain Sandstone

The mountains are capped by a belt of hard sandstone. This was formed over millions of years by rivers depositing layers of sand and mud on a flood plain. These deposits were 3 kilometres thick and sank under their weight and turned to stone. About 200 to 300 million years ago, North America crunched into Africa. The Cape Fold Belt Mountains were forced up out of the sea and Table Mountain was 'born'. Table Mountain stands out with its distinctive flat top but you can see dramatic folds in some of the other mountains.

Table Mountain Sandstone seen along Chapman's Peak Drive. Alternating layers of dark mud and pale sand were deposited on a flood plain by ancient rivers. The layers have been interrupted where a rift occurred and the rocks shifted up or down.

Oldest rocks – Malmesbury Shales

In some places even older rocks have been uncovered by erosion. The oldest, hard, dark rocks can be seen at Sea Point, jutting out into the waves. These mudstones and sandstones were laid down 560 million years ago in an ancient ocean and were later buckled and folded.

Ancient rocks, Malmesbury shales, about 560 million years old are weathered by the Atlantic Ocean off Sea Point.

Fiery origin – Cape Granite

About 550 million years ago, during earth collisions, balls of molten ooze (magma) rose towards the surface, melting and cracking the earth's crust. The magma cooled and crystallised into granite. Today huge, grey boulders of Cape Granite can be seen exposed by erosion on the flanks of Lion's Head and along the coast of the Cape Peninsula.

Granite boulders near Miller's Point. Crystals were formed as the molten magma cooled about 550 million years ago.

Amazing biodiversity

The range of life – biodiversity – in the Cape Floral Kingdom is richer than anywhere else on earth. Why should there be so many different species in this tiny region?

Endangered **geometric tortoise,** one of 6 tortoises endemic to the region

Explosion of species

The Cape Flora has been isolated from the rest of the world for millions years. Protea pollen is recorded from 95 million years ago. Since that time the southern tip of Africa has experienced hot and cold periods, floods and drought but the fittest, best-adapted plants have managed to survive. Recent research on fossilised pollen in sediments indicates that in the last 3 million years there has been a rapid increase in the number of species. A combination of isolation and periodic harsh conditions has led to the evolution of thousands of species that are uniquely adapted to the winter rainfall region of southern Africa.

A few of the thousands of different daisies, vygies and plants with bulbs that occur in the Cape Flora.

things to do

Look at the fields and mountain slopes in the Western Cape and you will find that they are covered with circular patches. These are called 'heuweltjies' or little hills. Thousands of years ago each hill was a termite nest. The termites, known as white ants, enrich and aerate the soil in their nests and create a new habitat. Notice how the plants that grow on the little hills are different from those between the hills. Together they create colourful patterns of circles.

A termite mound

Islands within an island

The tip of Africa is like an island surrounded on the south and west by oceans and bordered in the north and east by mountains and semi-desert (see map on page 59). The plants are further isolated from the rest of Africa because the south-western Cape has winter rainfall and its plants become dormant in summer when their northern counterparts are growing and flowering due to summer rain. This winter rainfall 'island' is itself broken up into little 'islands' by the nature of the mountains, the different types of soil, the altitude and different amounts of rainfall. So the plants adapt and inbreed within each different isolated habitat with little opportunity for cross-pollination or transfer of seeds between habitats.

Harsh selection pressures

In addition to the variations in habitat there are periodic harsh events that kill off weak plants so that only those that are best adapted can survive.

Winged adults fly off to start a new colony

Inside the mound

Termites are social insects

Dry summers

In order to survive, plants must be adapted to the hot dry summers. Many are succulents, or have small leaves, like the ericas and restios, or spend summer as seeds or underground bulbs (see pages 38–42).

Fire

Fire is another catastrophe that destroys the dry fynbos area and renosterveld. These veld types have many fire-adapted plants that survive underground as seeds or bulbs, or have woody fire-resistant bark and cones. Animals like ants, moles and even butterflies are also fire-adapted (see pages 36 and 48).

Restios (Cape reeds) with small leaves and waxy stems, are superbly adapted to winter rainfall and dry summers.

Smoke stimulates the seeds of fire ericas to germinate.

Soil nutrients

Weathering and erosion create soil. Granite and Malmesbury Shales form fairly rich soils but the sandy soil from Table Mountain Sandstone is low in many essential elements like phosphorus and nitrogen. Sandy soil also drains quickly and nutrients are easily washed away. The low nutrient content of the sandy soil has reduced most fynbos plants like ericas to low-growing evergreens that can retain their precious nutrients in small hardy leaves for years on end. Many of them also form partnerships with bacteria and fungi to help their roots absorb the scarce nutrients. These plants can easily produce sugars and starches by photosynthesis, so many of them have nectar and store starch.

Plant and animal interactions

The harsh conditions have also affected the animals, which are generally small or live underground. The vegetation is not very nutritious for large grazers or caterpillars. Bees, flies and beetles can, however, make good use of the nectar and pollen and their larvae do not eat leaves. The shortage of animals to aid pollination means that flowers have developed nectar and amazing colours and shapes to attract insects, mice and birds (see pages 14 and 34). Special partnerships have developed between plants, ants and butterflies to ensure their mutual survival (see page 36).

did you know?

Velvet worms are often called 'missing links' between worms and arthropods (centipedes and insects). Several different species can be found in the moist, leafy litter on the forest floor.

did you know?

This long-tongued fly sucks nectar from five different flower species, all pale pink with red markings. Together, the flowers provide enough food to sustain the fly that pollinates them. To avoid mixing their pollen, each flower type dusts pollen on a different part of the fly's body.

Ericas and sunbirds

During the summer, while walking in the fynbos, you are bound to see ericas or heaths. These are neat bushes with small leaves and clusters of dainty flowers with four petals joined to form a tube or cup.

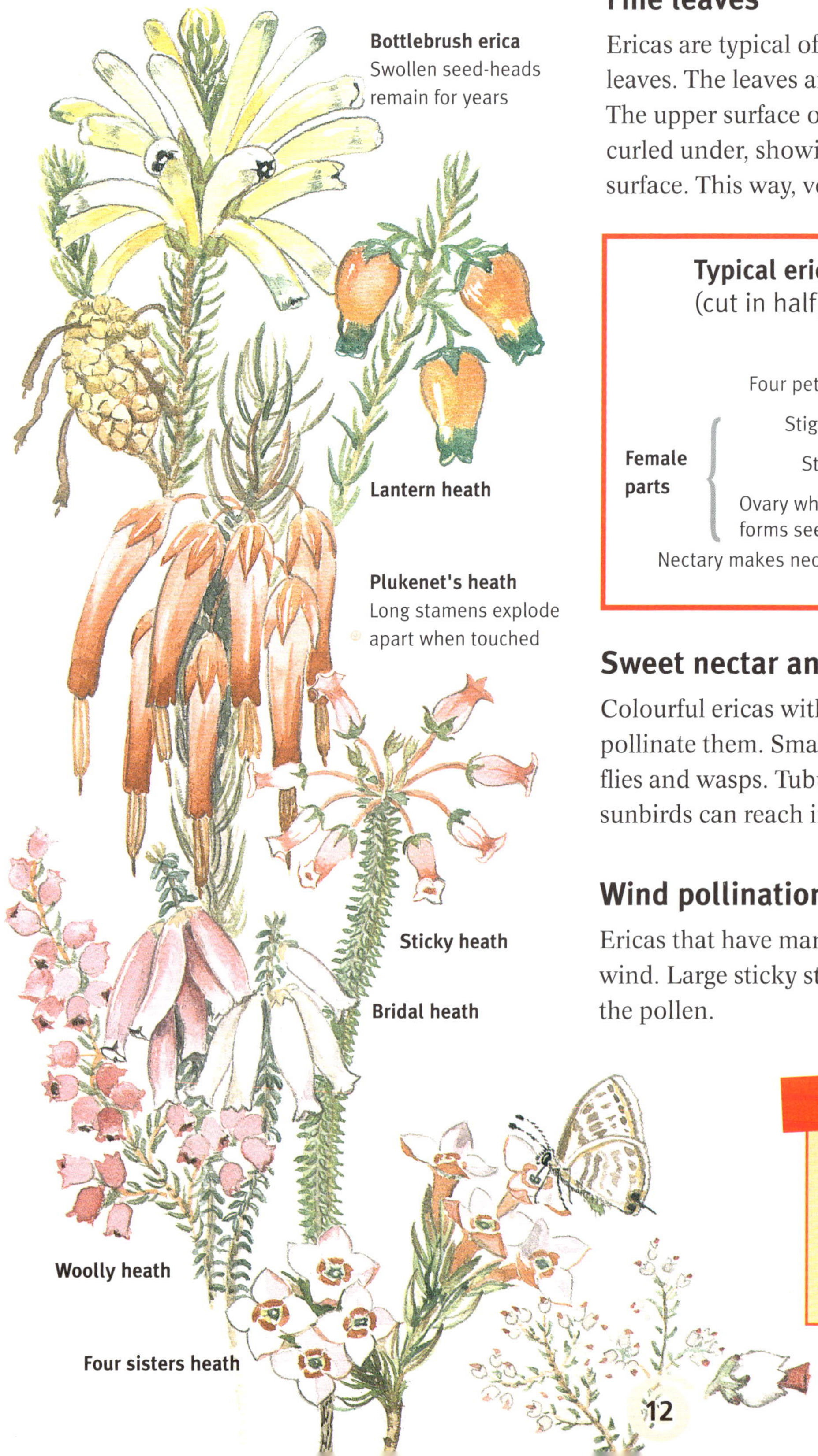

Fine leaves

Ericas are typical of Cape Flora fynbos because they have fine leaves. The leaves are shaped to cope with the dry summers. The upper surface of the leaves is waxy and the sides are curled under, showing only a small slit of the hairy lower surface. This way, very little water is lost through the leaves.

Typical erica flower with four joined petals (cut in half)

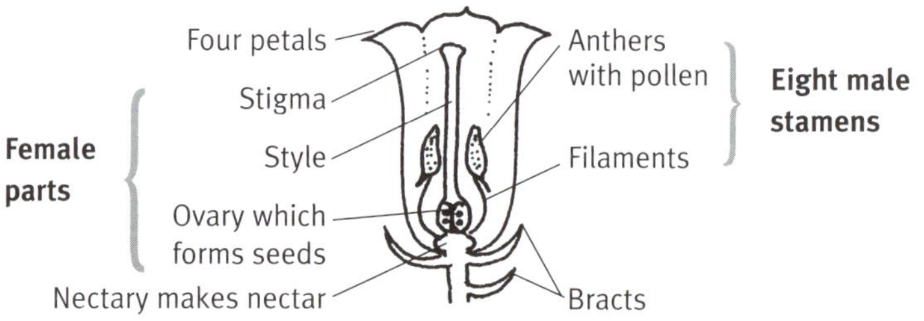

Sweet nectar and bright colours

Colourful ericas with sweet nectar attract birds and insects to pollinate them. Small, cup-shaped flowers are visited by bees, flies and wasps. Tubular flowers are specially designed so that sunbirds can reach inside with their long curved beaks.

Wind pollination

Ericas that have many small dull flowers are pollinated by the wind. Large sticky stigmas stick out of the flowers to catch the pollen.

things to do

It is a botanical mystery why there should be so many different ericas in the Cape. Don't worry if you have difficulty naming them all, rather enjoy their beauty. Start with the easy ones illustrated here.

Sunbirds

Male sunbirds dart about flashing their bright plumage and long tails and sing loudly from the tops of bushes. They challenge any other males that venture into their territory. The females are dull brown with short tails and are well camouflaged when they sit on their nests of twigs and leaves. They lay their speckled cream eggs on a soft lining of feathers and protea fluff. Sunbirds are rapid fliers requiring a lot of food. They swoop and catch insects, and use their forked tongues to drink the energy-rich nectar from ericas, proteas, aloes, watsonias and other tubular flowers.

Sunbirds eat insects and nectar. Bright male Lesser Doublecollared Sunbird

Dull female sunbird

Sticky rose heath
Bees visit cup-shaped flowers

Kapok heath
Hairy bracts discourage ants

Regal erica
Pollinated by sunbirds, robbed by carpenter bees and short-beaked birds

things to do

Make a chart of the ericas and record:

Flower shape	Sticky or hairy	Colour	Visitors	Robbers	Date
e.g	Sticky	Red	Birds	Bees	

Flower robbers

Fat carpenter bees and short-beaked birds, which cannot reach the nectar in the long narrow-tubed ericas, cheat and bite a hole in the side of the flower. They rob the flower of its nectar without carrying any pollen to other flowers.

Masson's erica
Hairy leaves and sticky flowers discourage insects and reduce water loss

Keeping robbers out

Many ericas have ways of stopping these nectar robbers. Some have large thick bracts at the base of the flower which stop insects from nibbling a hole in the base. This forces them to go to the entrance, where the pollen is. Other plants are hairy or sticky to prevent insects from crawling on the outside of the flower. Flying insects that transport the pollen for long distances can still enter the mouth of these flowers.

did you know?

Although ericas occur worldwide, there are over 500 different species concentrated in the Cape. Ericas belong to the family Ericaceae.

Proteas

People are fascinated by the unique beauty and variety of proteas. In the past they were also a vital source of wood and food. Early settlers around Cape Town discovered that if they placed the flower-heads of the common sugarbush protea face down, they could collect buckets full of sweet nectar to use as syrup, known as 'bossiestroop'.

Sugarbush, *Protea repens*

Proteas are bird tables!

Proteas produce lots of nectar, not for humans but for birds. The giant flower-heads act as fancy bird tables. The bright bracts attract birds and the clump of densely packed flowers in the centre provides a sturdy landing platform. Proteas supply all the needs of the Cape sugarbird. It not only sips the nectar with its tongue and long curved beak, but feeds on the insects and spiders that come to the proteas. The female sugarbird builds her cup-shaped nest in the protea bush and lines it with fluff from protea seeds. The long-tailed male chooses a high perch from which to survey his territory, and chases off any other males. The proteas benefit when the birds carry pollen from flower to flower, resulting in pollination and the production of seeds.

things to do

Sit quietly near some proteas. Listen to and watch the birds in action.

A **shy protea**, *Protea amplexicaulis*, is visited by a striped fieldmouse

did you know?

There are 69 species of protea in the fynbos. How many can you find? They belong to the family Proteaceae.

The mystery of the 'shy' proteas

For years botanists were puzzled as to how pollination took place in those proteas that have dull-coloured flowers hidden amongst the leaves at ground level. Then they noticed little footprints, droppings and nibbled bracts around the yeasty-smelling flowers. At night they caught mice with protea pollen on their whiskers and fur. In the laboratory they were able to watch and photograph the mice drinking nectar from a flower. However, they couldn't be sure that these shy nocturnal creatures transferred pollen from one flower to the next.

In the wilds the scientists dusted one flower with fluorescent powder and waited. Later, when they examined the area with ultraviolet light, the powder glowed, revealing paths running from the treated flower to other nearby flowers where the powder had been brushed off while the mice fed there. So we now know that several proteas are pollinated by mice.

South Africa's national flower, the giant or king protea, *Protea cynaroides*, reaches 30 centimetres across. It is recognised by its colour and long leaf stalks.

The waboom, *Protea nitida,* is a small tree with corky fire-resistant bark. Its wood was used for building wagon spokes and furniture. Water condenses from mist onto the broad waxy leaves and helps it to survive the long dry summer.

Protea beetle

Proteas are African

Proteas occur only in Africa. Of the 117 protea species more than half are clustered in the Cape Floral Kingdom. The land here is separated into pockets by the mountains and proteas have become specialised to survive in these restricted habitats. For example, four different forms of the giant king protea have developed in isolated areas. This is a step towards becoming new species as these forms have different-shaped leaves and flowers, and they flower at different times of the year so they cannot pollinate each other. To find the largest most beautiful king proteas you need to climb to the tops of mountains in summer. Near the sea, the flowers are small and spiky to cope with gale-force winds.

things to do

How many insects and spiders can you find on proteas?

Pincushions

'Pincushion' is a good name for these colourful balls. There are 48 different species of pincushion, or Leucospermum. Like proteas, they belong to the family Proteaceae and look like the centre of a protea without its bright bracts.

'Pins' for pollen presenters

The pincushion is a collection of many small flowers each with its own 'pin'. In the centre of a young flower head, you will see that the 'pins' are curved over with their tips clasped by four joined petals. The male anthers sit inside the swollen tips of the petals and coat the pinhead with pollen. When a bird lands on a pincushion and probes for nectar with its beak, the petals split apart and the 'pin' springs up and dusts the bird with pollen. These 'pins' are called pollen presenters. Once the pollen has been removed, the tip of the pollen presenter splits and becomes the sticky female stigma, ready to receive pollen brought from another flower by a bird.

Sunbirds as pollinators

Dainty sunbirds are welcome pollinators of pincushions. The friendly Orangebreasted Sunbird is found only in the Cape and can easily be spotted darting around when the fynbos is in bloom. Lesser Doublecollared Sunbirds (see page 13) and green Malachite Sunbirds visit the Cape in summer and autumn to feast on the nectar and insects they find in the flower-heads. Sugarbirds (see page 14) also visit pincushions but are bigger, and rather rough and can damage the flowers, so are better suited to the sturdier protea.

Single pincushion flowers

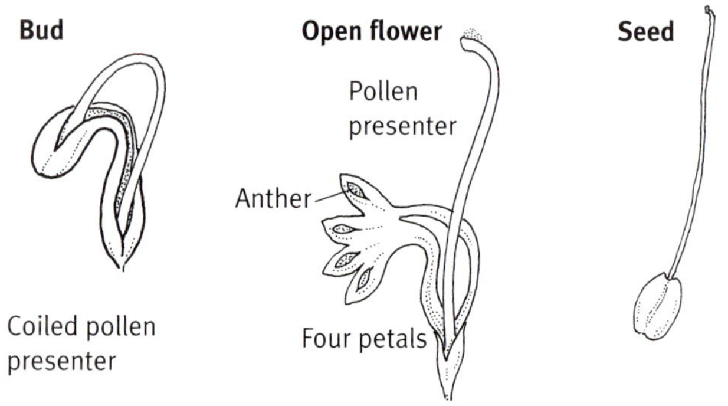

Insect visitors

Many insects also come along for a meal. Some, like the protea beetle, help in pollination but other smaller creatures slip between the pins without collecting any pollen. They are, however, an extra source of food for sunbirds.

An **Orangebreasted Sunbird** perched on a common **orange pincushion**

things to do

Count how many little flowers there are in a single pincushion head. Later, see if you can count how many seeds are produced by the same or a similar head. How good was the pollination? You may need to cover the old dried flower with a paper bag so that birds such as doves can't take the seeds.

things to do

Examine how the pollen presenters work on a pincushion and a serruria.

This serruria-of-the-valley looks like a strange pincushion but has branching, needle-like leaves. It is a relative of the blushing bride (see page 50).

Growing pincushions and proteas

Most pincushions and proteas grow best in a sandy acid soil that is well-drained. They don't like manure but do well in compost or if pine or wattle leaves are scattered around them. It is important to know where the plants come from and what conditions they experience in nature. For example, the south-western Cape has winter rain while the south-east coast has rain all the year round. On the flat coastal plains the rainfall is about 300–500 millimetres a year, but in some mountain kloofs the rainfall is as high as 3 000 millimetres a year. Proteas and pincushions have special shallow roots with tufts of tiny roots at their ends, so don't dig the soil around them. If you plant protea seeds not all of them will grow at once – some will only germinate a year or two later, while others will never grow at all!

things to do

Look at the seeds on an old yellow kreupelhout flower. Perhaps baboons think they look like bloated ticks on a hairy animal! That is why they are known as 'luisies' in Afrikaans.

The yellow kreupelhout is a common gnarled bush found growing on mountain slopes near the sea. The red rocket pincushion has grey hairy leaves.

The pincushion is a head of tiny flowers. The pollen presenters are held like coils by the tips of the petals and stick out when they are older.

The leaves of the pincushion are broad and usually have teeth at the tips, which makes it easy to tell them from protea and serruria bushes, even when there are no flowers.

Flower farming

To grow flowers that sell well throughout the year, farmers use the seeds from only the most beautiful plants and destroy those with dull flowers to avoid cross-pollination. They also select plants that flower at different times of the year. If some of the tip buds are removed side branches develop resulting in better flower production over a longer period.

Silver trees and sunshine proteas

If you have ever stroked a silver leaf, kept one as a book-mark, or watched the silver tree glistening in the wind, you will understand why the Table Mountain silver trees are now grown all over the world. The scientific name *Leucadendron argenteum* means 'white tree silver'. Sunshine proteas that are small yellow and red bushes are also species of *Leucadendron*.

Useful silver hairs

The fine hairs on the silver tree's leaves can move. They stick out in wet weather so that air can circulate around the leaves, but when it is dry they lie flat against the leaf and help reduce water loss.

Silver trees grow to a height of 8 to 10 metres. They may die suddenly when attacked by a fungal disease that lives in the soil.

things to do

Look out for farms like 'Silverhurst' and 'Witteboom' that have been named after silver trees.

Colourful sunshine proteas.

Sunshine proteas

In addition to the silver tree there are nearly 80 other leucadendrons, which are not 'white trees', but the yellow and red-tipped bushes that brighten the mountain slopes. It is fun to look at the cones of different types of sunshine proteas and try and match up the male and female plants. They are very popular for use in flower arrangements and are also attractive when they are dry.

Guinea fowl scuffle amongst the leaves for insects and seeds. They nest on the ground but roost at night in trees, where it is safer.

did you know?

The family Proteaceae includes the proteas, pincushions, leucadendrons, serrurias (of which the blushing bride is the most famous), mimetes, aulax and a few others (see pages 14–17 and 50). Their flower-heads are made up of similar tiny flowers with pollen presenters. Hakea, a pest tree from Australia, also belongs to the Proteaceae (see page 52).

Mimetes

Mimetes are red- or yellow-leafed plants, often called 'stompies' because the straight stalks have flat tips with a cluster of leaves that look like a glowing cigarette end. One species in particular even has bunches of pollen presenters with black tips that look just like matches. Unlike Leucadendrons, mimetes do not have separate male and female plants.

Feather duster

Aulax, the feather duster flower, has bright yellow feathery male flowers and cones on the females. They grow well near Hermanus.

things to do

Examine the thickened tips of mimete leaves. They produce nectar to attract ants. How do you think the ants could benefit these plants? (see page 37)

did you know?

There are male and female silver trees.
Although silver trees were first described in 1620, it was over a hundred years before botanists realised that there are separate male and female trees. The male tree has a pompom of tiny flowers surrounded by a rosette of leaves and produces the pollen. The female tree has cones with nut-like seeds, which the squirrels love to eat. The cones open when they are ripe and strong winds shake the trees and carry the seeds away, hanging from neat parachutes. The feather duster and sunshine proteas also have male and female bushes.

Cone from female **silver tree**, sweetly scented

parachute seeds of silver tree

Pompon flower of **male silver tree**

Red male and yellow female of ***Leucadendron discolor***

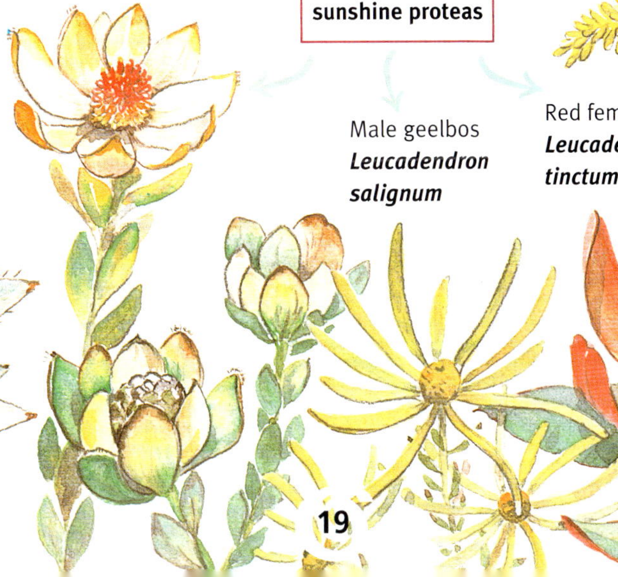

sunshine proteas

Male geelbos ***Leucadendron salignum***

Red female ***Leucadendron tinctum***

Bontebok and Cape reeds

Can you imagine life as a buck – relaxing in the shade of a tree and nibbling the soft end of a grass stalk? Yet in the Cape there are very few shady trees and, instead of tender grasses, there are clumps of stiff Cape reeds. This area does not carry the huge herds of animals that live in the grasslands of Africa, and those that were once here have moved away or were hunted to extinction.

Bontebok

did you know?

There is an unusual national monument about 10 kilometres from Bredasdorp on the road to Arniston: a section of the historic ship-rail fencing used for the first bontebok reserve.

Bontebok

The bontebok is endemic to the Cape where it used to graze between Bot River and Bredasdorp. But they were such easy targets for hunters with their white faces, white socks and rumps, that they almost became extinct, like the quagga and blue antelope.

Fortunately, the wise owner of a farm called 'Nacht Wacht', at Bredasdorp, collected 27 bontebok and in 1837 established the first nature reserve to protect them. He fenced it with metal rails salvaged from ships that had been wrecked along the treacherous coast near Cape Agulhas. In 1931 some of these bontebok were taken to the new Bontebok Park at Swellendam. Today there are more than 1500 bontebok countrywide and they are unlikely to become extinct.

things to do

Find out how many nature reserves in the Cape have herds of bontebok. Visit one of them and notice the single males that occupy prominent spots. How do they behave when other males arrive? The females wander in the males' territories whereas the young males are excluded and form bachelor herds.

Cape reeds (restios) make long-lasting thatch used in Khoikhoi mat houses, fishermen's cottages and gracious Cape Dutch homesteads

The **blue crane** is the national bird of South Africa. It stands a metre high and is easy to recognise, with its smooth swollen head and long black-tipped wings that hang down like a tail when folded. Blue cranes can be seen eating seeds and insects in open grass and wheat lands.

Cape reeds – restios

The Cape reeds belong to the family Restionaceae, and are known as restios. Their presence helps us to recognise fynbos vegetation. They are wonderfully adapted to the climate and grow well when swamped by winter rains, and in baking summer heat. Unlike grasses, their leaves are small, dry and brown. Their stems are green and have taken over the function of the leaves. They have separate male and female plants and a fascinating variety of little cone-like flowerheads.

things to do

Look out for the yellow orb-web spider and the grey bark spider that weave their beautiful webs between the restios. Have they caught anything in their webs?

Yellow orb-web spider with a neatly packaged fly.

things to do

Compare restio flowers, leaves and stems with those of grasses. Which is the bunnytail grass? Its leaf is folded around the stem and flattens out into a soft green blade.

Cape reed (restio)
female flowerhead with feathery stigmas

Cape reed (restio)
male flowerhead with pollen

Wind pollination

The male flowerheads of restios produce lots of light pollen that is dispersed by the wind and settles on the feathery stigmas of the female flower-heads (see page 33).

Geraniums and pelargoniums

Pink pelargoniums brighten the coastal villages of Chile in South America and cascade from baskets hanging on lamp posts in Canada. More than 35 million pelargoniums are sold by nursery gardens in America each year, while in France they are grown for their perfume. Often incorrectly called geraniums, most of the world's pelargoniums are originally from the Cape.

The hooded-leaf pelargonium is a hardy shrub that grows all over the Cape. The flowers are faintly scented and attract sunbirds, bee-flies, butterflies and moths.

The hairy leaves of the hooded-leaf pelargonium are folded to shade one another and reduce wind movement so that they don't dry out during summer.

Comparing geraniums and pelargoniums

True geraniums are cup-shaped, with five similar petals and ten fertile stamens. Pelargoniums usually have two large upper and two or three small lower petals. Not all of the 10 stamens in the pelargoniums have anthers on their tips. Over 400 species of pelargonium occur in South Africa.

Hybrids – improving on nature

Gardeners produce new hybrids of pelargoniums by cross-pollination. They take the pollen from one species of pelargonium and use it to pollinate another. The plants that result from the seeds are a mixture of the characteristics of the two original species. These new mixed plants are called hybrids. Gardeners carefully select the most beautiful hybrids and multiply them by taking slips or cuttings from them and growing new plants. The result is that many of the pelargoniums that are grown in gardens are hybrids with bigger, brighter flowers than the wild species.

Herbal leaves

The leaves of pelargoniums may be smooth and succulent, soft and hairy, coarse and rough or even feathery like a carrot leaf but in all of them the veins of the leaf come from a central point, like the fingers of a hand. The leaves may be scented and some are used as herbs, teas or medicines to treat headaches and diarrhoea.

things to do

Crush and smell the leaves of different pelargoniums. Visit the fragrant garden for the blind at the National Botanical Gardens at Kirstenbosch. Feel and smell the leaves. There are lemon, rose and cinnamon-scented pelargoniums.

The true geranium, known as 'bergtee' is used to make herbal tea. Its petals are all similar and the seed pod looks like a miniature maypole.

The seed pod is the clue to the family Geraniaceae

The young pods look rather like birds' heads with long beaks. The name pelargonium is a Greek word meaning 'stork's head', while geranium means 'crane's head'. The dry pod looks like a maypole with the seeds hanging out from the central stalk on fine threads. Pelargoniums, geraniums and monsonia belong to the family Geraniaceae because they have similar seed pods.

things to do

Examine the seed pods of a pelargonium. Place some loose dry seeds on damp sand or tissue paper and see how they twist around. This action helps to drill the seeds into the soil where they land.

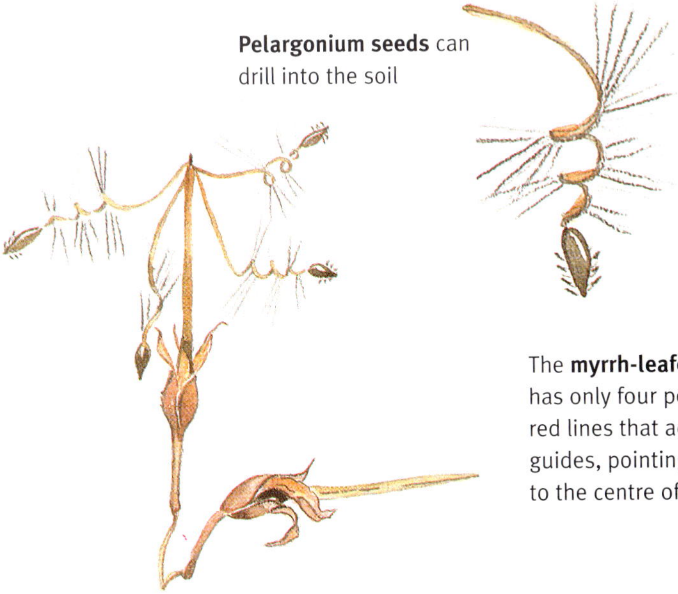

Pelargonium seeds can drill into the soil

The **myrrh-leafed pelargonium** has only four petals. These have red lines that act as honey guides, pointing insects to the centre of the flower

The butterfly flower, monsonia

things to do

Many pelargoniums grow easily from slips. Stand a piece of stem in water and after a few weeks you will see roots growing from the stem. Slips can also be planted directly into the garden. To stimulate the roots to grow more quickly the cut end of the slip can be dipped into a 'rooting hormone' before planting. This hormone is available from garden shops.

Nature's bulb garden

The Cape Flora grows as a wonderful natural garden of infinite variety. Apart from the fynbos perennials there are the 'surprise plants' that sprout from underground bulbs and corms. These are known as geophytes. Most geophytes are monocotyledons, like lilies and orchids. This region has the richest geophyte flora in the world.

A watsonia in 'nature's garden'.

Lion's Head – a wild garden

When the English botanist William Burchell first visited Cape Town in 1810 he climbed Lion's Head, the hill near Table Mountain. There he counted over 100 different plants in a distance of one kilometre. He wrote in his diary that he found it hard to believe that such a wonderful garden could have been planted purely by nature. Today 'nature's garden' can be seen in all its glory in only a few unspoilt places, but the flowers are grown in gardens throughout the world.

things to do

Count how many different plants you can find on a walk of one kilometre.

Amazing hybrids

Sometimes wild flowers in gardens are better than in nature, as a gardener, Japie Krige, discovered in 1930. He planted red *Sparaxis grandiflora* from Tulbagh next to orange, yellow and white, *Sparaxis elegans* from Nieuwoudtville. Insects cross-pollinated them and when he collected and grew the seeds he got twelve magnificent hybrids with different patterns and colours. In just a few years he had hundreds of beautiful blooms on show in his garden. These two species would never be cross-pollinated in the wild because they are separated by large mountains. Today there is a thriving bulb industry selling hybrids from wild Cape flowers.

Multiplying hybrids

The seeds of a hybrid, if it produces any at all, are not guaranteed to grow into the same lovely flowers as their parent. Fortunately, there are other ways of multiplying hybrids to produce new plants exactly the same as the parent. A cutting may be taken from the hybrid and grown (see pelargoniums on page 23), or bulbs and root clumps can be split to make more plants. These methods of reproduction that do not involve pollination are called vegetative reproduction. The plants shown here all have bulbs or corms, which are swollen food stores.

things to do

Compare wild flowers with their hybrids in gardens.

Painted lady gladiolus

Wine cups

Ixia

Three hundred years ago a ship bound for Holland with nerine bulbs was wrecked off Guernsey in the English channel. The bulbs survived and became known as Guernsey lilies, but their real home is Table Mountain.

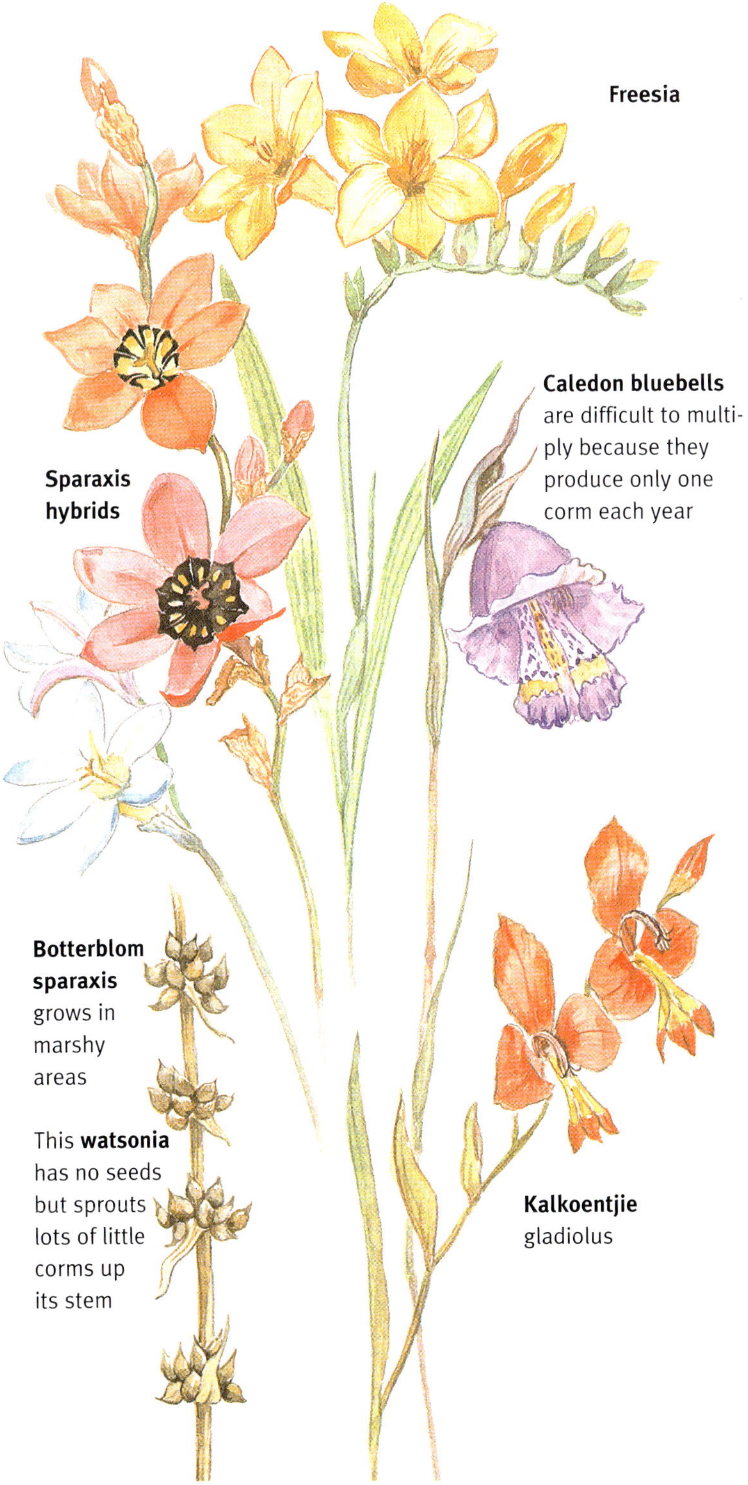

Freesia

Caledon bluebells are difficult to multiply because they produce only one corm each year

Sparaxis hybrids

Botterblom sparaxis grows in marshy areas

This **watsonia** has no seeds but sprouts lots of little corms up its stem

Kalkoentjie gladiolus

things to do

Use the clues in the table below to tell whether plants are monocotyledons or dicotyledons.
The two large groups of flowering plants are:

Monocotyledons	**Dicotyledons**
A One seed leaf (cotyledon) e.g. mealie 	**A** Two seed leaves e.g. bean 
B Leaves with parallel veins 	**B** Leaves with net veins 
C Flower parts in threes or multiples of three e.g. Star flower 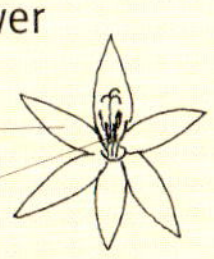	**C** Flower parts in fours, fives or more e.g. Erica (heath) 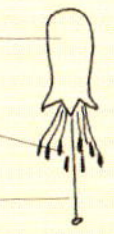
D Stems not woody	**D** Stems may be woody
E Often have swollen bulbs or corms underground	**E** Bulbs and corms rare

(All the flowers shown on this page are monocotyledons with six petals and leaves with parallel veins.)

things to do

Start a collection of plants that grow from bulbs or corms and see if you can make a plant calendar. For example, freesias flower in September, chincherinchee (page 39) in October, March lilies (page 49) in March and nerines in April.

Daisies

Daisies are spectacular examples of the sandveld flowers that survive the harsh dry summer as seeds and then burst into flower in spring. They do well in areas that have been cleared of natural vegetation, so you can see fields of white rain daisies or banks of yellow Namaqualand daisies and purple wild cinerarias growing along the roadsides.

A beetle daisy crowded with black spots that were thought to mimic beetles. Find out below what really happens.

White rain daisies and yellow Namaqualand daisies spring to new life after rain.

Daisies are real sunlovers

Daisies only open fully on a bright sunny day and they turn their faces to follow the path of the sun. In overcast or wet weather they close up, protecting their pollen. Each daisy is really a whole head of tiny flowers surrounded by bright petals. Daisies belong to the family Asteraceae which is one of the largest plant families with many thousands of species.

Annuals and perennials

Many daisies are annuals; the plant dies after flowering but new plants grow again the following year from seeds. Others are perennials which grow as small permanent bushes for many years.

did you know?

Scientists have recently solved the riddle of why beetle daisies have black markings. They have nothing to do with beetles but mimic black bee flies. The flies zoom into the flower, attracted to the dark spots, and find nectar and possibly a mate.

The pink everlasting is a perennial with tiny leaves and a woody stem. The papery petals dry without losing their colour.

Button daisies have small petals or no petals at all, and cannot close in dull weather.

Purple wild cineraria.

Daisy seeds

Look at different daisy seeds. Some have parachutes like delicate papery stars, while others have tufts of long hairs. The dune flower has thorny seeds that hitch a ride on animals. The wild rosemary or 'kapok' bush has fluffy seeds that are spread by the wind and collected by birds and mice to line their nests (see page 36). Many daisies produce two types of seeds – one that germinates the following year and one that waits for longer and germinates in later years.

Insects come for the pollen

Daisies are pollinated by insects, mainly bees and beetles, which eat the pollen and so most daisies do not produce nectar. Beetles are attracted by yellow, so many of the flowers are yellow or orange or have yellow centres. The monkey beetle (see page 55) often uses its long back legs to hold a daisy petal over its back for shade or to hide from birds. Some daisies have markings like a target, to lure insects to the pollen.

things to do

Travel north-west from Cape Town on a sunny spring day and feast your eyes on the daisies. Notice how different daisies prefer particular areas. Some like the dunes, others grow in ploughed fields, some live in stony soil, others in wetter areas. See how many of the 2 000 different daisies you can find. Note how the leaves differ. Make sure you have the sun behind you so that you see into their bright faces.

Beetle eating pollen of a dune daisy.

Vygies – Midday flowers

Vygies look a little like daisies with brilliant, shining flowers. They have the most amazing seed capsules and are succulents with fleshy leaves or stems that can store water.

Dazzling purple vygies open at midday. Each is a single flower unlike the yellow daisy which is a whole head of tiny flowers.

Midday flower

Vygies belong to the family Mesembryanthemaceae – 'mesembs' for short – which means 'midday flower'. This is because most of them open at midday, in bright sunshine, to attract insects. Some with yellow flowers stay open right into the evening. In the centre of each mesemb flower is a branching stigma with lots of little stamens around it.

Pale vygies may stay open right into the evening. The leaves have bulging cells that store water and act as light-controlling lenses.

Succulent leaves

Look at the fleshy vygie leaves that store water. In some species the leaves have bulging transparent cells on their surface that sparkle like grains of sugar. They act like lenses, controlling the amount of light that reaches the tissues beneath. They are sometimes called 'ice plants'.

did you know?

There are over 2 000 different types of mesembs in South Africa. Most occur in the drier desert areas of the Namib and Karoo but they are also common in the dry sandveld of the south-western Cape. They include the fascinating stone plants (see page 43).

Dry, closed seed capsules

A wet, open seed capsule

Dried sour fig fruit

things to do

Place the dry brown seed capsule of a vygie in water and watch it open like a beautiful star. It is one of the most complicated fruits in the plant kingdom. Raindrops landing on the open capsule bounce the little seeds out and they are washed away. As soon as it dries, the capsule closes again to protect any seeds that are left. By releasing a few seeds at a time there is a better chance that some will survive and grow, even if the rainfall is unreliable.

Amazing colours

The shine of the petals is caused by pyramid-shaped cells in the surface layer which concentrate and reflect light. The colours are so vivid that when photographs were first sent to Europe, the printers toned down the colours because they thought there had been a mistake. Vygies, like daisies, have no scent or nectar and use bright colours to attract pollen-eating insects.

The perennial bosvygie uses water from its succulent leaves to survive the hot dry summer.

things to do

Split open a fleshy sour fig and taste it. Boil sour figs with sugar to make jam.

The huge purple-flowered sour fig grows well in sand near the seaside. Its soft edible fruits have hundreds of little black seeds in a sticky sour syrup. The name 'vygie' means 'little fig'.

things to do

Plant some bokbaaivygie seeds. They are very small and light. About 70 000 seeds weigh only one gram. They grow easily and give a sparkling display in a sunny place. If the soil is too rich they tend to have lots of leaves and only a few flowers.

Bokbaaivygies are multicoloured annuals. With the onset of rain they grow, flower and die back within a few weeks. They spend the dry season as seeds enclosed in fancy seed capsules.

Food and fresh air factory

People rave about the spring flowers on the West Coast after a good rainy season. However, on my first trip, a drought year, all we found were dried bones and shrivelled aloes – stark reminders of the importance of water for life.

All healthy plants need sun, water and air.

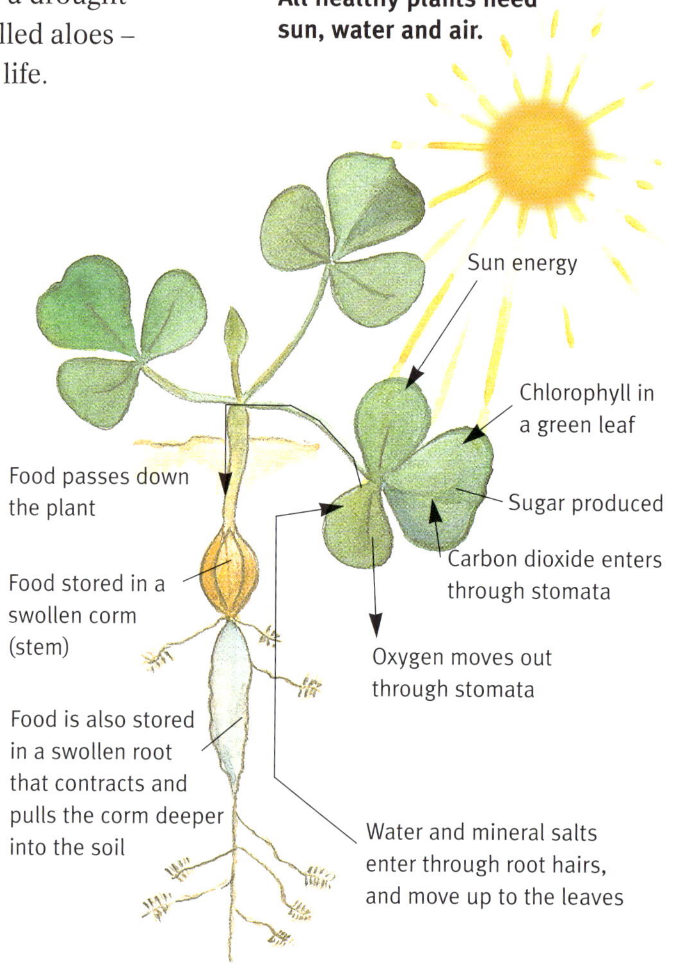

Why is water so important?

About 60 per cent of any plant or animal (including humans) is made up of water. Plants can do something special with water that animals cannot do – plants can make sugar from water!

Making food by photosynthesis

The leaves of the plant are like a factory: their green colouring is a chemical called chlorophyll, which captures energy from the sun. Plants use this energy to make sugar from water and carbon dioxide from the air. This chemical process is called photosynthesis. The plants can then combine the sugar with nitrogen and mineral salts to make other body-building materials like proteins. The water and mineral salts for the process are collected from the soil by the roots, which have fine hairs to increase the surface area for absorption. Water travels up the plant in narrow tubes to the leaves. Air enters the leaves through little 'windows' called stomata which can be opened and closed.

Photosynthesis
water + carbon dioxide —(chlorophyll, sunlight)→ sugar + oxygen

Respiration
oxygen + sugar ——→ carbon dioxide + water + energy

Sorrel (Oxalis) grows like a weed. The sour leaves of sorrel contain oxalic acid.

Plants act as an 'air freshener'

During photosynthesis plants remove carbon dioxide from the air and return oxygen. We breathe in the air and use the oxygen for energy and change it back to carbon dioxide, which we breathe out.

A network of veins carries food and water inside the leaf.

things to do

Find out about food chains in nature. For example:

- A plant is eaten by a dassie which is captured by a black eagle.
- A daisy is eaten by a tortoise whose blood is sucked by a tick.

Animals need plants

All animals depend on plants for their food. Some animals are herbivores, like tortoises, caterpillars and dassies. They feed directly on plants. Carnivorous animals get their food indirectly from plants by feeding on animals that have eaten plants.

Check for ticks

After walking in the veld always check for ticks or you might become part of a food chain. When a tick sucks your blood it may infect you with a parasite that causes tickbite fever.

Dassies

Dassies love to bask in the sun but are ready to dive into rocky caves at the approach of danger. They have long sensitive hairs in their thick fur which stand out and act like whiskers to help the dassies feel their way in the dark. Dassies have short legs and rubbery soles to their feet which sweat to give them a good grip as they clamber over rocks. Baby dassies are born covered with fur and with their eyes already open. They are able to run around within a few hours of birth.

In mountainous and hilly country dassies need to be continually on the look out for the majestic black eagle. One female dassie acts as the crier and calls if danger approaches. The eagles often hunt in pairs. One soars in the open and, while the dassies watch it, the other swoops around the cliffs and grabs a dassie with its talons.

A tiny **speckled padloper tortoise** eats a beetle daisy. Tortoises bury their hard-shelled eggs in the sand where they take up to 14 months to hatch.

Eagles and farmers

Eagles can live for 20 to 30 years and have no natural enemies other than farmers, some of whom, misguidedly, shoot them. Although eagles sometimes kill young lambs, they are in fact farmers' friends. A pair of eagles will eat 350 dassies in a year and restrict the dassies to rocky ledges where they can hide. Where there are no eagles the dassies move onto the plains and 350 of them will eat enough food to support 22 healthy sheep. Lambs are usually taken by young inexperienced birds, so it is better to have resident adult eagles that will keep young birds out of the area. If farmers rear lambs near the homestead and far away from the eagle eyrie, the benefits of the eagles will far outweigh any losses.

Eagles use the same eyrie to nest in each year. It can be up to a metre wide. The fluffy white chick grows and is taught to tear its own food from the carcass. Under the watchful eye of the parents it finally learns to fly.

Flowers and pollination

When we marvel at the lovely colours, scents and shapes of flowers we forget that they were not made for our pleasure but to help the plant make seeds. The earliest plants had no flowers and grew from spores, like ferns and mosses do today. For thousands of years it was a mystery as to how flowering plants made seeds.

How pollination was discovered

About 200 years ago Jeremiah Grew discovered that pollen must reach the stigma before a flowering plant can make seeds. He thought that the pollen from a flower landed on the stigma of the same flower.

A hundred years passed before this hypothesis was questioned. C K Sprengel was puzzled by the position of stamens and thought it seemed unlikely that pollen could fall on the stigma of the same flower. It was as if the flowers were actually trying to prevent self-pollination. Then he noticed that insects visiting flowers for nectar were dusting pollen onto the stigma. The idea that insects and flowers work together caused a revolution in science. But he still thought that insects passed pollen to the stigma of the same flower.

Christmas berry flower – note how the stigma is held separate from the stamens to prevent self-pollination.

The red stigma is situated above the stamens in hibiscus flowers and they ripen at different times to prevent self-pollination.

things to do

Choose a flower and work out where the stamens and pollen are. Find the stigma which may be sticky or hairy. How is the plant adapted to encourage cross-pollination and prevent self-pollination? Check whether the pollen is shed before the stigma is sticky, or at the same time.

Pollination and fertilisation

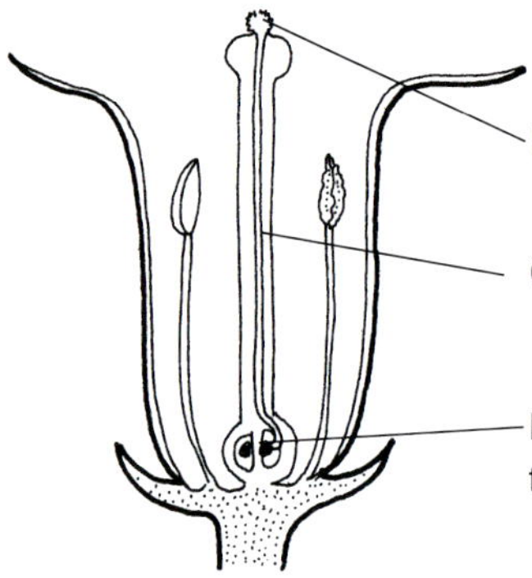

Cross-pollination and fertilisation

We now know that most flowers are cross-pollinated. During cross-pollination the pollen of one plant is transferred to the stigma of another plant of the same kind. The pollen (male cell) then grows down the stigma and fuses with the ovule (female egg cell) in a process known as fertilisation. The male and female characters are mixed so that the new plants are a little different from the parents (in the same way children have a mixture of their parents' features). It is an advantage for plants to have variations in their offspring as a result of cross-pollination. It helps them adapt to different conditions, spread into new areas and even evolve into new species.

Sexual and vegetative reproduction

Pollination and fertilisation are necessary for sexual reproduction in flowers. However, plants can continue to grow, and even spread, without sexual reproduction by using special underground shoots, roots and corms. The new plants produced in this way are exactly the same as the parent plant. This is called vegetative reproduction (see page 24).

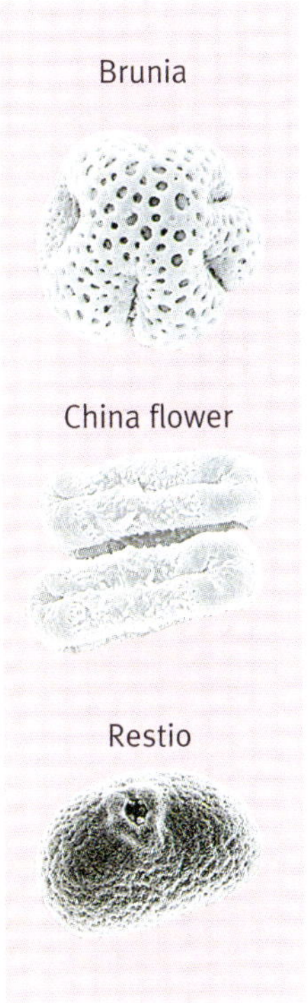

Pollen grains magnified over 500 times.

Pollen grains – microscopic gems

Pollen is the fine powder produced by the male part of the plant. It is different for each type of flower. Pollen will only grow if the stigma on which it lands is of the same species, and gives the correct chemical signal. Brunia, the China flower, and many other flowers have rough pollen that clings to animals that visit the flowers. Restio pollen is light and is carried between the flowers by the wind.

things to do

Look on the back of a fern or bracken leaf for the groups of spores. Try growing some in a mixture of leaf mould and pieces of broken brick. Stand your pot in a tray of water and cover it with glass or plastic to make sure it does not dry out. Ferns grow well in a terrarium (see page 55).

things to do

See how many different-coloured pollens you can find. What is the most common colour and why?

The scented pepper and salt flowers have contrasting dark and light colours that are noticed by insects.

Flowers advertise their wares

Birds, insects, mice and even bats are lured to flowers by the promise of nectar and pollen for food. The flowers use scent, bright colours, and contrasting patterns to advertise themselves. Insects can detect ultraviolet light and see colours differently from us. I wonder how they see the pink romulea and purple lapeirousia? Small flowers make more impact if they are grouped together and open one after the other (see pincushions and daisies on pages 16 and 26).

The sweet scent of *Hermas villosa* draws insects to the ball of pale flowers.

The pink romulea and purple lapeirousias have 'arrows' pointing to the pollen.

Brilliant red crassula flowers grouped to attract attention.

Insect pollination

Flowers have evolved amazing shapes to increase the chance of successful pollination, particularly by insects.

things to do

In January and February, hike in the mountains and keep an eye open for the spectacular red disa orchid which grows in wet places next to streams. They were once quite common.

Nivenia with long stamens

Long-tongued fly

Nivenia with short stamens and a long stigma

Pollen can be wasted

Plants that rely on the wind have to make loads of light pollen in the hope that some of it will be blown to the right stigma. Pollen is also wasted when animals visit several different flowers and the pollen is dusted off on the wrong flower. Open flowers like daisies can be visited by a whole range of insects and are successfully pollinated only because they grow in dense groups.

Bees

Bees are excellent pollinators because they visit only one kind of flower at a time. They also call out other bees from the hive to come and collect nectar and pollen. There are many different kinds and sizes of bees and most of them do not live in swarms like honey bees.

Nemesias

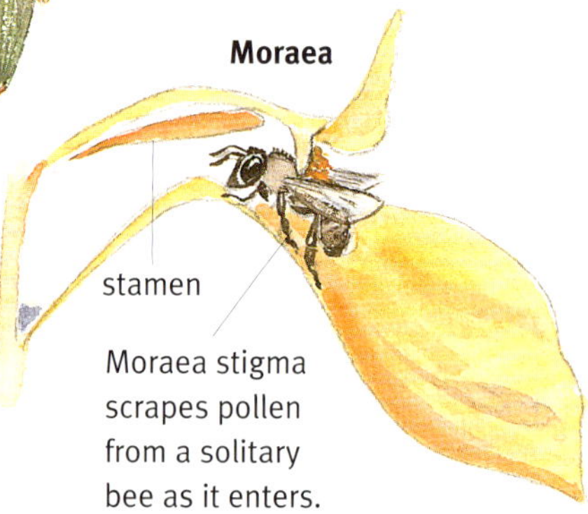

Moraea

stamen

Moraea stigma scrapes pollen from a solitary bee as it enters.

Flowers shaped for bees

To improve pollination, some flowers are shaped to let in bees of a certain size only and to keep out other insects. Nemesias, lobelias and salvias have closed flowers with a landing platform. When the bee lands, its weight lowers the petal and opens the flower so that the bee can push its way past the anthers and down to the nectar. The anthers of the salvia are hinged and swing down to dust the back of the bee. The stigma of the moraea flower forms a flap that scrapes pollen off a body of the bee as it enters. The bee is then dusted with new pollen and the flap closes as it leaves, carrying this pollen to another flower.

Lobelia

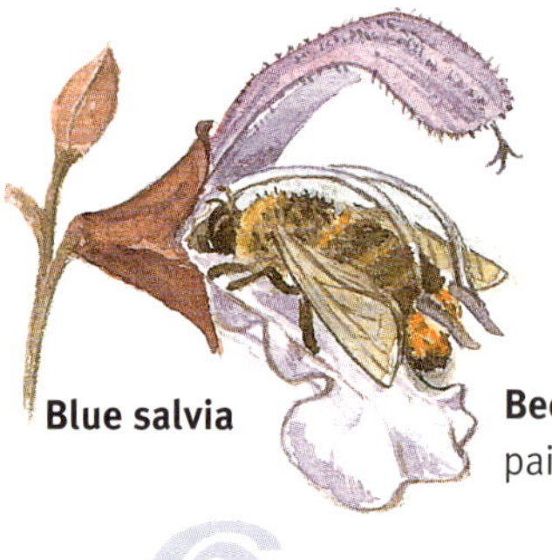

Blue salvia

Bees have two pairs of wings

Long-tongued flies and nivenia

A long-tongued fly hovers in front of a tubular nivenia flower, sipping nectar with its long tongue. Nivenias have two types of flower to ensure cross-pollination. One has long stamens and a short stigma while the other has a long stigma and short stamens. When the long stamens dust the body of the fly, the pollen can be carried to the long stigma of the next flower. The short stamens dust the face of the fly which later touches the short stigmas of another flower.

Long-tongued flies are useful in another way: their larvae eat the eggs of locusts and so reduce the danger of a swarm of locusts eating acres of crops.

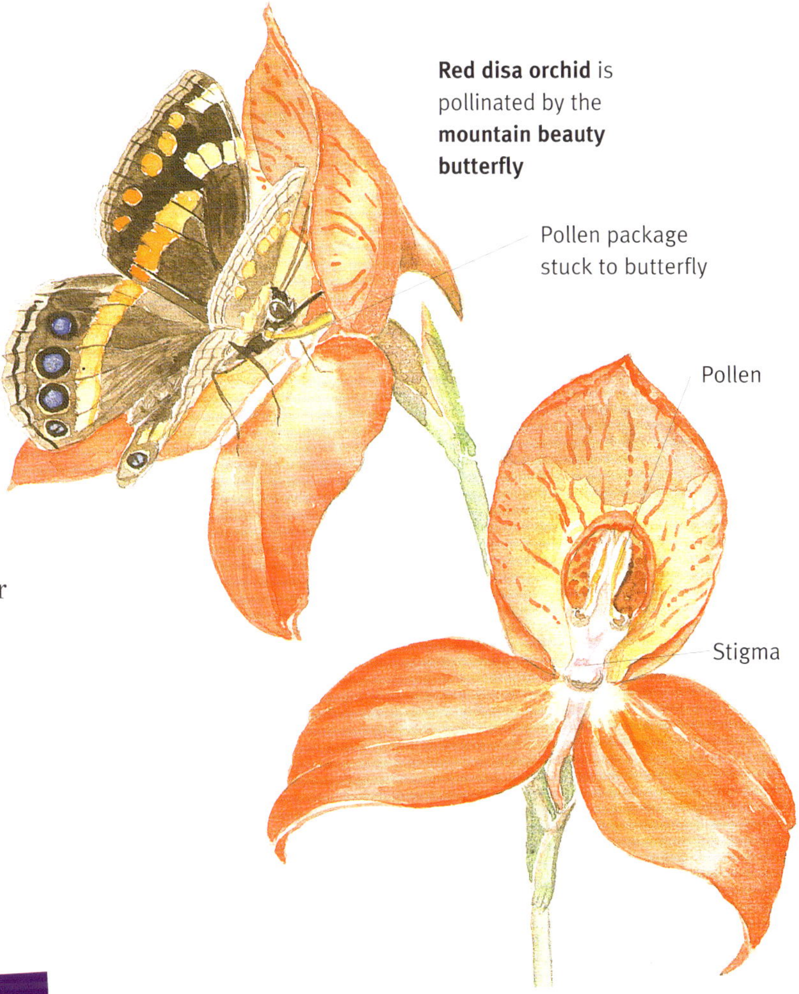

Butterflies are active pollinators

Butterflies uncurl their long tongues to feed on narrow, long-tubed flowers. In February, mountain beauty butterflies visit red disa orchids and in April they feed on red nerines. Their different flowering times prevent the butterfly from mixing their pollens.

Painted lady butterfly sips from **drumstick flowers**

things to do

Try and work out how flowers are pollinated. Watch for visitors and other clues:

- Bees often come to yellow or purplish-pink flowers that have dark honey-guide lines. They see ultraviolet light so the colours look different to them.
- Pale, sweet-scented flowers are visited by moths at dusk.
- Birds prefer red and orange flowers, and need a firm perch to sit on while they feed.
- The dull flowers of grasses and restios are wind-pollinated.

Matter of taste

Some flowers have developed smells which attract specific pollinators. The stapelia or carrion flower smells of rotten meat. Flies zoom in to feed and their legs slip into special grooves in the centre of the flower. As they struggle free they hook out neat packages of pollen which stick to their legs.

Seeds that walk and fly

Daisy parachute seeds

Plants are usually anchored to one spot by their roots. However, their seeds travel in amazing ways to colonise new areas. They can fly, parachute, use wheels, hitchhike or even be carried along underground trails to their new destinations.

Bush willow seed

Agapanthus winged seed

Candelabra seed-head rolled by the wind

Seeds carried by the wind

The tip of Africa, once known as the 'Cape of Storms', is famous for its gales. All sorts of seeds fly in these winds. The blue and white agapanthus has light seeds with a flattened wing. Cape bush willow seeds have four wings, while those of daisies and silver trees drift down on dainty parachutes. The large dried head of the candelabra flower rolls over the veld like a ball, dropping seeds as it goes

Candelabra flower, *Brunsvigia*, flowers in March.

Juicy fruits

The seeds found inside juicy fruits have a hard coating that allows them to pass right through the birds that eat them and grow later in a new place. The fleshy seeds of autumn-flowering plants do not have a dry resting period. They grow immediately and make the most of winter and spring rains. In summer they rest underground as bulbs. Examples are April fools, candelabra flowers, March lilies and nerines (see pages 25 and 49).

Thorny hitchhikers

Thorny seeds hitch an unwelcomed ride on feet and bicycle tyres. Those of the yellow dune daisy have leafy wings and a thorny centre so they can use both the wind and animal transport. Kapok bushes and proteas have fluffy seeds that are collected by birds and mice to line their nests.

April fool, *Haemanthus*, has red flowers. The fleshy seeds are folded down when the flat leaves grow.

Yellow dune daisy

Kapok has fluffy seeds

Cape grey mongoose limps off with a thorny satin flower seed in its paw. It feeds at night on insects, eggs, mice and even snakes.

Satin flower seed

Ants help fynbos seeds

Scientists were amazed to discover how little ants acted as seed carriers. Many of the fynbos seeds have fleshy, oily caps. Moments after a seed has dropped to the ground, tiny ants team up to drag it to their underground nests. They then nibble off the fleshy part, discarding the hard seed. In the ant nest the seeds have a better chance of surviving fires and escaping from seed eaters. When the conditions are right the seeds germinate in the enriched soil of the ant nest.

Ants as butterfly babysitters

Ants also play a fascinating role in the life of the small lycaenid butterfly. While the young caterpillars are feeding on plants they are visited by ants that collect sweet drops from a gland near the caterpillars' tails. Later, these ants carry caterpillars down into their nests where they are cared for and even allowed to eat the ants' own larvae. The caterpillars remain below, safe from fire, birds and wasp or fly parasites. There they pupate and later the butterflies crawl to the surface and fly off. Lycaenid butterflies, often known as blues, are common small orange or blue butterflies with a tiny tail on the hind wing (see also page 12). Some lycaenid butterflies like the Brenton blue are endangered because their special habitat is being destroyed.

things to do

Find some Acraea caterpillars on a wild peach tree and keep them to see what sort of butterfly they turn into. You may find some have been parasitised by wasps. The wasps lay their eggs on the caterpillars. Their larvae live inside the caterpillar and crawl out to pupate. The wasp's grey and black cocoon hangs by a thread from the dried caterpillar skin.

things to do

Place small pieces of meat near an ant nest. If narrow columns of ants stream over it, they are the alien Argentine ants that have been introduced from South America. They chase off the local ants and eat the seed coats but unlike the local ants they do not carry the seeds to safety below ground.

things to do

If you tread on a thorn, try to find the culprit plant. It may be the common three-spined devil thorn.

Cape White-eye eats the fleshy orange seeds of the **wild peach tree**

Birds do not eat the poisonous **Acraea caterpillar**

Cocoon of a wasp parasite on an Acraea caterpillar

Lycaenid butterfly (see also page 12)

Ants carry a lycaenid caterpillar into their nest

Ants collect seeds

Caterpillar eats ant larva

Seed store

Moles and geophytes

Moles burrow underground and are very common mammals in the Cape. Mole rats feast on bulbs and push up mole hills. Golden moles run along just below the surface of the soil, eating insects and worms.

The Cape dune mole rat

Mole rats are not easy to study and it can take days to dig up and follow the burrows of a huge Cape dune mole rat, which can be the size of a rabbit. The burrows run 30 centimetres below the surface and are about a third of a kilometre long. In the burrow is a nest lined with grass and leaves. Mole rats pull roots and whole plants underground and eat them there.

things to do

Use a bucket to measure how much soil there is in a single mole hill. Count how many new mole hills are produced in a day within a fixed area. Estimate how much soil the mole rat has removed from its burrow – is it a small truckload?

Dig open the top of a fresh mole hill and feel inside to see how big the tube is. In a short while, the mole will plug up the opening again.

The Cape mole rat

This smaller mole rat digs with its curved front teeth – these keep growing as the tips are worn away. It shovels the soil backwards out of the mole hill. The Cape mole rat collects a food store of bulbs and corms. Only one Cape mole rat lives in each burrow. When a male and female want to meet and mate they send vibration signals by drumming with their hind feet.

Mole snakes

Underground, the mole is safe from fire and most predators. However, as soon as fresh soil is turned up, mole snakes slither along to investigate. These large, dark snakes have a small head and a pale belly. They are not venomous but squeeze their prey to death. They help to control the huge populations of moles. Moles snakes are quite common and give birth to about 40 little snakes in April.

Chincherinchee flowers last for six weeks in a vase. The bulbs are very poisonous.

did you know?

Moles undermine roads, railway lines and air strips causing them to collapse. Special mole barriers and traps are used to try and solve the problem.

Geophytes store food underground

Geophytes are plants that spend part of the year underground as swollen bulbs or corms and so survive the dry summer season and veld fires. They can also store scarce mineral salts to pass on to next year's plants. Corms were the staple diet of the early Khoisan people and are a wonderful source of food for baboons, porcupines and mole rats. For their defence many geophytes are poisonous. For example, chincherinchees, moraeas and homerias often cause the death of sheep and goats, when their leaves are harvested with hay. But mole rats happily eat the poisonous bulbs and survive.

Bulbs can benefit from moles

One food store of the Cape mole rat that was dug up contained 4 944 corms and bulbs! Yet some geophytes, like micranthus, are adapted to living with mole rats. Instead of a single corm they produce a cluster, or have small corms higher up on the stalk. When the mole rat carries off one corm to eat, the others are scattered along its path, survive and are spread into new areas.

Cape golden mole

The small Cape golden mole is common in many gardens in the region. It is not a mole rat. It makes runs just below the surface of the soil and gobbles up its own weight of insects and earthworms every day. Unlike mole rats, it does not eat bulbs or have long curved teeth, and is totally blind but very sensitive to vibrations.

Parasites and sundews

Some parasitic plants cheat and do not make their own food by photosynthesis. Instead, they latch onto the roots or stems of other plants and absorb the ready-made food from their host plants. They can then put all their energy into producing beautiful flowers and vast numbers of seeds.

Inkblom

The pale flowers of the inkblom absorb their food from the roots of ericas and other host plants. It is often difficult to work out which plant is their host plant. No wonder they are not common garden plants, in spite of their lovely flowers. They turn black when bruised and have been used to make ink.

Cat's nails

The velvety snail flower, Hyobanche, has always fascinated people and has been given many interesting names. 'Cat's nails' refers to the flowers from which the stigmas stick out like claws. The fleshy fruits are eaten by animals, especially tortoises, and so it is sometimes called 'skilpadkos'. Its underground stem latches onto the roots of a host plant and only the flower bursts out of the sand dunes where it lives.

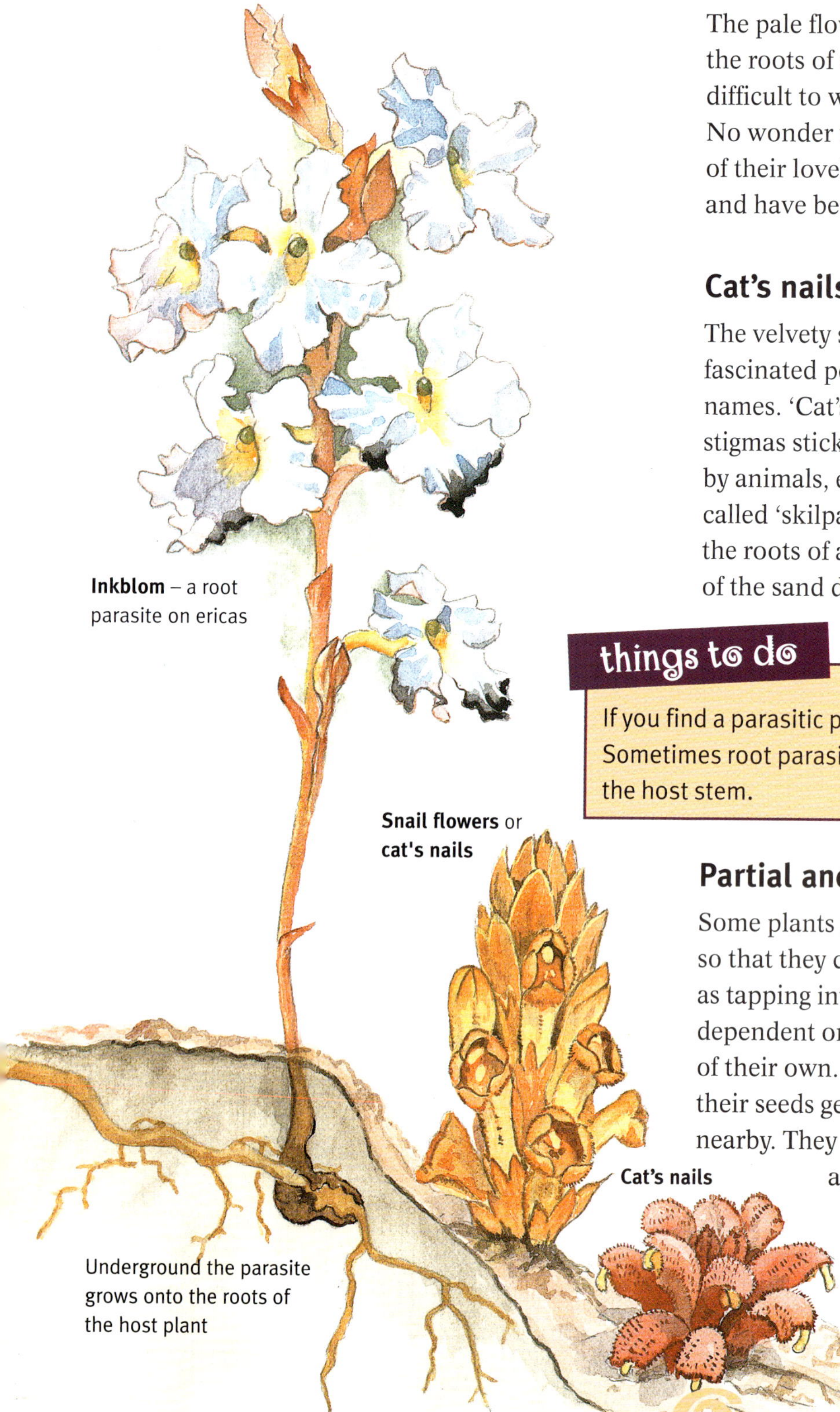

things to do

If you find a parasitic plant try and find its host plant. Sometimes root parasites grow some distance from the host stem.

Partial and total parasites

Some plants may be partial parasites. They have leaves so that they can make some of their own food as well as tapping into the host's supply. Others are totally dependent on the host plant for food and have no leaves of their own. When this is the case it is important that their seeds germinate only where there is a suitable host nearby. They produce lots of seeds which can wait for ages and grow only when they are stimulated by a chemical from the roots of a host. Birds eat the red berries of witches tresses and drop the hard seeds which can lie dormant for years.

Tapping of a host's supplies

Witches' tresses hang like matted yellow threads from plants. Wherever they touch a plant a little pad develops, the tissues of the host plant are dissolved away and the parasite links up with the tiny tubes in the plant that carry the sap. This is like connecting a side pipe to the plant's water system.

How does the parasite 'turn on the tap' to get the sap flowing through its own tissues? When water evaporates from the leaves of a plant the cells become floppy, like a balloon that is going down. Water moves in from a full cell next to it, which in turn becomes floppy and draws water from its neighbour and so on, all the way down the plant to the roots which suck water out of the soil. If a plant loses more water than it can suck up it will become droopy and wilt and its stomata close. This suction pull is called transpiration pull. A normal plant tries to avoid losing water but the parasite has many stomata openings through which a lot of water evaporates. The transpiration pull is thus greater in the parasite and so the sap flows into the parasite, which grows quickly, at the expense of its host.

Witches' tresses

things to do

Look for sundews. They often occur in damp places. There are several species with different-shaped leaves and delicate flowers. Try feeding one with a live insect.

Plants that eat insects

Sundews attract insects to the sparkling red hairs that cover their leaves. When insects land they are trapped by the sticky drops, and the hairs curl over and glue them to the leaf. They are digested by the leaf and then absorbed to provide scarce nutrients.

This red-flowered sundew has long leaves. The yellow flower is the bloodroot. Both live in swampy areas.

The sticky drops on the leaves of the sundew are used to trap insects.

Leaves and drought

In winter rainfall areas, where the summers are harsh and dry, it is interesting to see the different methods that plants use for survival. Fynbos plants have small leaves to reduce evaporation while succulents store water. Other plants die down and spend summer as bulbs or seeds.

Hairy arctotis bud.

A grasshopper on katstertjie (Struthiola). The small leaves are held vertically.

Spittle bugs nest in bubbles of plant sap from a slangbos.

Phylica has small, curled hairy leaves.

Cancer bush has grey compound leaves.

Fynbos leaves reduce evaporation

While we enjoy summer weather, the fynbos is under stress and would shrivel and die if its leaves were not well adapted to these conditions. Fynbos leaves tend to be small and often have a waxy, waterproof covering but they must still have pores (stomata) to allow air to enter for photosynthesis. To prevent too much water from being lost, these stomata are often placed on the lower surface of the leaf where they sit in shady hollows, surrounded by hairs to reduce air movement.

Fynbos plants have adapted in various ways to avoid drying out. For example, the summer flowering arctotis occurs in dry areas and has very hairy leaves. The leaves of ericas and phylica curl so far under that the sides almost meet, creating a hiding place for their stomata. The babiana, spiloxene and the hooded pelargonium all have pleated leaves to minimise the surface area exposed to the sun. The grey leaves of the cancer bush are split into many leaflets that can fold, and which are also less likely to be damaged by strong winds. Many leaves are silvery grey so they reflect sunlight and do not get too hot.

The plants also tend to point their leaves to the sky so that only a small surface is exposed to the hot midday sun. The edges of these leaves may be protected by hairs, or are red to mask out the burning rays of the sun. The leaves of pincushions have thick tips (see page 16).

did you know?

Deciduous plants like oaks and vines shed all their leaves in autumn. Evergreen plants bear leaves all the year round and use the scarce nutrients as long as possible. Their leaves must withstand the heat of summer and the cold of winter. Fynbos and succulents are evergreen.

Steenbok get all their water from the plants they eat. They hide their lambs in holes in the ground. If disturbed the adults zigzag away and then stop and look back with their ears held out. The male has short straight horns.

things to do

Choose three areas with different levels of rainfall and compare the size, colour and surface coverings of the leaves found in them.

Succulents store water

Succulent plants store water in their swollen leaves or stems to tide them over the dry season. The water is usually combined with chemicals in the sap so that it does not evaporate easily.

Aloe with swollen, bitter, spiny leaves.

Animals and succulents

Large and small animals rely on these fleshy leaves for their survival. However, succulents are well adapted to avoid being eaten. Aloes are bitter tasting and have spines. Pig's ears and euphorbias have poisonous sap. The stone plant is small and grey with speckled markings and hides camouflaged among stones during summer. When the winter rains come, the outer skin splits, fresh green leaves and bright vygie flowers then grow to attract pollinators.

things to do

Breed the African monarch caterpillar until it becomes a red, black and white butterfly (see page 2). The pupa is pretty with a gold-beaded necklace. They feed on poisonous plants and become distasteful to birds.

What is in the water?

Wetlands are very important habitats. If you look closely you will find that they are teeming with water-loving plants, insects, frogs, fish, birds and other animals. They are rich feeding grounds for migratory wading birds that fly all the way from their breeding grounds in Russia and Canada.

Water lilies

What a pity the Cape water lily has become so rare. Its flowers, which close at night, are beautiful when reflected in a pond. The flat leaves float on the surface of the water. Their stems are spongy with lots of air spaces to carry air down to the underwater stems and roots. Another flowering water plant is the fast-growing Cape pondweed, or waterblommetjie. Its two-horned flower-heads with black stamens have a sweet scent. They are delicious when added to mutton stews.

things to do

Look for tadpoles in streams. See if you can find any that have developed legs, the final stage before becoming a frog.

Platannas and frogs

The platanna or clawed toad lives in water all the time. Unlike the river frog, it has no eyelids, eardrums or long tongue for catching flying insects.

Arum lilies

In wet and boggy places you will find arum lilies with their trumpet-shaped flowers. The large leaves of the arum have special water stomata that stay open all the time to get rid of extra water. When these leaves are warmed they can be used as a poultice to treat boils and sores. Fleshy berries develop in the old flowers and are eaten by birds. Porcupines dig up and eat the fleshy underground tubers. But be careful of the sap because it contains needle-like crystals that will irritate your mouth and it will leave a permanent brown stain on clothes. Arum lilies are now grown in many other countries where they are known as calla lilies.

The crab spider and arum frog

The crab spider and the little arum frog wait patiently to capture insects that are attracted to the musky smelling flowers of the arum lily. The frog is pale cream in the sun but will become quite dark in the shade. This varies the amount of heat that the frog absorbs, so that it can control its body temperature. It has bright orange legs which flash a warning to startle predators.

did you know?

Platannas were once in great demand and thousands were shipped around the world to be used in the only reliable test for pregnancy. If a little urine from a pregnant woman was injected into the female toad it laid eggs the next day and confirmed that she was pregnant. Luckily a new test was found and platannas were left in peace.

things to do

Look under the leaves of the arum lily for hawk moth caterpillars. It is fun to feed them until they pupate and turn into hawk moths.

Hide and seek

The animals in the pond are playing deadly hide-and-seek. Can you find them?

1. Whirligig beetles spin in the water. Their eyes are split in half so that they can see both above and below the water at the same time.
2. Water striders walk on the surface of the water.
3. A water snake is harmless to humans.
4. Dragonflies eat other insects.
5. Dragonfly nymph – swims, catches mosquito larvae and becomes a dragonfly.
6. Damsel flies look like dainty dragonflies but with folded wings.
7. Arum hawk moth caterpillars change colour before pupating.
8. A white crab spider patiently waiting for a fly.
9. An arum lily frog shoots out its tongue to capture the fly.
10. Striped Cape river frog.
11. Swimming platanna.
12. Tadpoles are baby frogs.
13. Praying mantis.

Arum lily

Fire

Fire is such a powerful force. It is both exciting and terrifying to watch the crackling flames consume the dry veld. They scorch and destroy the plants and drive panicking animals before them. The heat and choking smoke add to the danger of trying to bring the flames under control. Fires can be sparked off by lightning, but more often they start from an unattended braai or a glowing cigarette butt.

Cape vulture

After a fire

If you walk through the disaster area after a fire, with puffs of ash rising at each footstep, you will feel a great sadness to see the destruction. Empty tortoise shells, burnt nests and charred bones are a reminder of the life that was there. Yet what a surprise awaits, if you visit a burnt area two or three weeks later. Beautiful fire lilies and April fools have appeared as if from nowhere to bloom in the ashes. Watsonias, pink March lilies, orchids and tulps flower later. You may even discover new plant species, like the two that were found at Greyton after a fire.

things to do

Follow the recovery of vegetation after a fire by visiting a burnt area every few weeks. Gradually, the lilies are crowded out by ericas and restios and finally, over the years, proteas will reach maturity and bloom again.

How plants survive fire

Fire is vital for the survival of many fynbos species (see blushing bride on page 50).

'Resprouters'

First up after the fire are the fire lilies. The fire stimulates their underground bulbs to grow. Some of them will lie dormant for over 20 years if there is no fire. Many of the plants shoot from underground corms or thick woody roots. The waboom has a thick corky bark that acts like a fire jacket. The young shoots are burnt off but new leaves sprout from the older tough stem and branches, and grow vigorously. Plants that resprout in this way can survive even if fires occur every few years. Fynbos leaves rot very slowly when they fall but fire releases their plant food and the ash becomes a fertiliser.

'Reseeders'

Other plants are killed by fire and must regrow from seeds. The seeds are either fire resistant or survive underground in the safety of ant nests. Some fire-resistant seeds remain on the plant in woody, fireproof cones and are only shed when the plant dies. The smoke stimulates hundreds of little seedlings to grow, but they must then have time to flower and set new seeds before there is another fire. Certain plants flower in their first year of growth while others, like the bearded protea, need at least seven years. Some even take 15 to 20 years. Because of this, frequent fires can wipe out fynbos plants that grow from seed.

did you know?

Fynbos and renosterveld are very well adapted to cope with fire as long as it occurs in summer. Fires in winter and spring destroy sprouting bulbs and seedlings and can kill birds while they are nesting.

Do not start fires

Only 'braai' in safe places and make sure the ashes are quite cold before you leave. Do not allow anyone to throw glowing cigarettes out of a car window. If you see a fire starting, act quickly by throwing sand or water on it. Call for help.

things to do

Decide whether plants are reseeders, with one stem growing out of the ground from a seed, or resprouters, with several shoots growing from a stump.

Valuable Cape plants

Many people recognise the value and importance of preserving the unique Cape Flora. However, it is not easy to manage these complex ecosystems and some surprising discoveries have helped to shape conservation policies for the region.

Saved from extinction

Delicate pink blushing brides are a great favourite in bridal bouquets. Few people realise how close this lovely plant came to extinction, and how blushing brides played a vital role in showing how the Cape Flora should be conserved.

Blushing brides were first recorded by Carl Thunberg, a Swedish botanical collector, in 1773 but mysteriously vanished for 110 years. There was much excitement when a cluster of plants was found in the Franschhoek mountains. With great care, seeds were grown and nurtured at Kirstenbosch Botanical Gardens. But the plants in the wilds dwindled until by 1962 not a single plant could be found in the protected area. It was with relief that a few scraggly plants were found some distance away, but an accidental fire swept through the area and destroyed them. However, to everyone's surprise, the seeds of the blushing bride were stimulated by the fire and fresh, healthy plants sprang up.

Blushing brides were saved from extinction

A new conservation policy

A new attitude to plant protection was born. Botanists realised that it is not enough to protect an area. It is important to understand the ecology and needs of the plants for them to be conserved. Today we know that many fynbos plants are fire-adapted and so controlled burning is used in nature reserves and by wild flower farmers. The fires should be set in summer at intervals of 15 or 20 years, depending on the plants present.

things to do

Plant some blushing bride seeds – they flower after only 15 months. In nature they grow on mountain slopes in clay soils where the annual rainfall is over 1 000 millimetres.

Wild flower farming

Wild flowers are farmed for both their fresh and dried flowers and their bulbs and seeds. There is a thriving export industry for proteas, pincushions and brunias because their striking flowers last for weeks in a vase and are a novelty in other countries.

Herbs and medicines

Not all important plants are spectacular. Some dull-looking plants are used as herbs and medicines. The Khoisan people were the first to discover these remedies and today many South Africans benefit from medicines made from indigenous plants.

The bruised tips of the grey renosterbos, *Elytropappus rhinocerotis*, are used as a tea or in brandy or wine to cure indigestion and diarrhoea. Buchu is the name given to a whole group of scented plants with oil glands dotted on their leaves. The most important are *Agathosma* and *Adenandra* species. They are drunk as a bitter tea or with brandy to cure digestive and kidney disorders. The thick extract obtained from soaking them in vinegar provides an ointment for sprains and arthritis. Everlastings, *Helichrysum* species, are excellent insect repellents. Pillows stuffed with the hairy grey foliage can be used to prevent asthma attacks (see page 55).

Rooibos tea

Rooibos is the basis of a thriving tea industry with a large export market. It is a 'health tea' with a high mineral content but lacks the caffeine found in other teas or coffees. Rooibos, *Aspalathus linearis*, is a plain bush of the pea family, grown in the mountains of the Cederberg and western Cape. The tips of the bushes are harvested, bruised and then fermented with a little water for 8 to 24 hours, before they are dried.

A bunch of *Brunia albiflora* flowers ready for export. They last for weeks and are still attractive when dry.

did you know?

Proteas have to be sprayed with insecticide before they can be exported because insects and mites hide in their fluffy centres.

The bearded protea, *Protea neriifolia*, was the first South African plant to be illustrated in 1605.

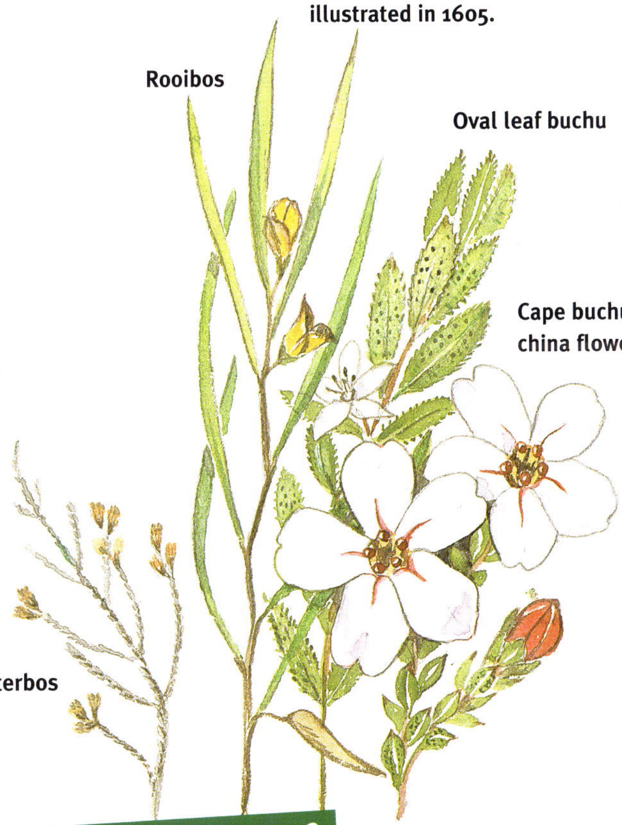

did you know?

At Kirstenbosch a unit has been established to cultivate and conserve plants used by traditional healers. They have also initiated community-based nurseries so that the wild populations of medicinal plants are not over-exploited.

Aliens on the march!

The magnificent isolation enjoyed by the Cape Flora came to an end when people deliberately imported plants and trees to the Cape. Most of these are beneficial but a few have become problem plants competing with the fynbos and greedily using up the water.

The introduction of foreign trees

In the Cape of 1680 there were few trees large enough to supply building timber for the growing settler community. At Tokai, foresters tried to grow many kinds of trees that they had brought from other countries. People were delighted by shady oaks but they grew too quickly to produce good wood. Port Jackson and rooikrans wattles from Australia settled the sand dunes so that travellers no longer had to battle through sand storms to cross the Cape Flats. A thorny hakea hedge would keep farm animals from straying. Cluster pines were a good source of wood.

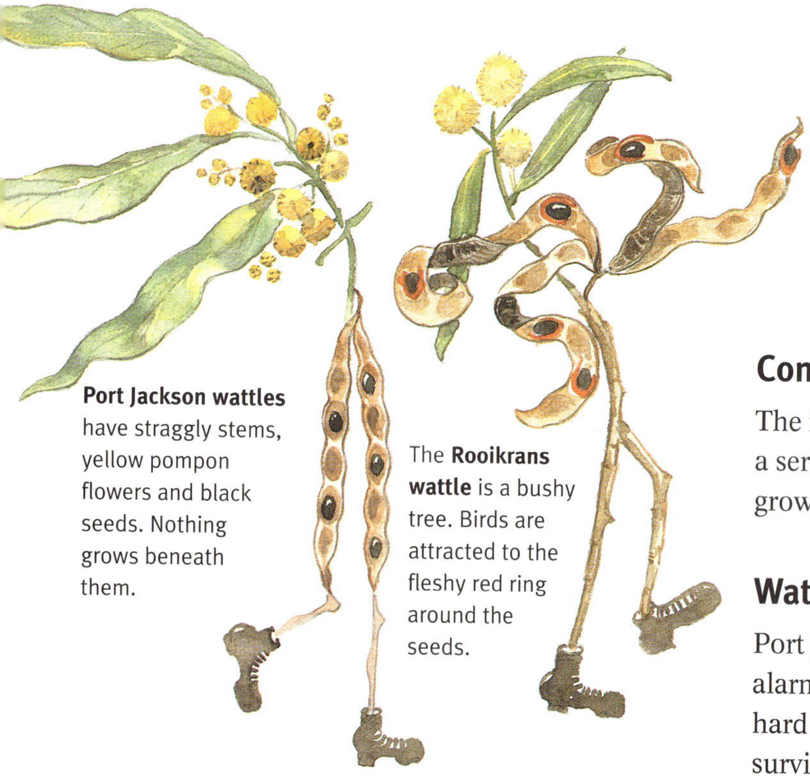

Conservation problem

The introduction of these alien plants has resulted in a serious conservation problem. Some of these plants grow too well and have crowded out the fynbos.

Wattle thickets take over the Cape!

Port Jackson and rooikrans wattles have spread alarmingly in sandy areas. There can be 10 000 of their hard seeds in one square metre of sand and they can survive and germinate after many years. The best way to get rid of the seed store is to fell and burn the trees. Some seeds are killed instantly by the fire while others survive and are stimulated to grow and must then be weeded out every two years. A new thicket will regrow within seven years if a single plant is left!

things to do

Get to know the pest plants – a book called *Plant Invaders* will help you (see page 61).

Hakea and pines climb the mountains

By 1970 hakea and cluster pines had smothered one third of the mountain fynbos. Hakea seeds do not drop but stay on the plant, enclosed in woody cones. Each year more cones are added. A single hakea tree can hold as many as 40 000 seeds. If the trees are cut or burnt to try and get rid of them, the cones split open and the winged seeds drift off to grow into even denser forests.

Pine emperor moth

What can be done?

Each pest plant has to be studied to work out the best way to control it. When scientists visited Australia they found only a few hakeas there, because insects were eating the seeds. So these seed weevils were brought back to South Africa and after careful testing were released in all the mountain ranges. In six years they destroyed four-fifths of the seeds in the experimental areas. Other insects and fungi that control hakea are also being tested to make sure they do not attack fynbos as well.

things to do

Join a 'hack' group. A seedling removed in time may save hundreds of rands and many hours of hard chopping!

Control measures

The best control for hakea is a combination of weevils, cutting and burning. The trees are cut in summer and release their seeds when they die. The seeds lie around for several months and many are eaten by birds and mice. The area is then burnt after about eight months to kill the young seedlings that have sprouted. Using this method, one-fifth of the infested area was cleared in 10 years and it seems possible that hakea can be contained but it is an ongoing battle. See also on page 57.

things to do

Examine the roots of a wattle seedling – they have swollen nodules where bacteria use nitrogen from the air to make fertiliser. This helps wattles grow more quickly than fynbos.

Biological control

Biological control is the use of a living plant or an animal to kill a pest. Scientists have to be absolutely sure that an introduced insect will not kill useful plants as well as the pest plant. For example, caterpillars of the pine emperor moth are no good for control because they eat fynbos and useful pines but avoid the cluster pine. However, gall wasps attack only the long-leafed wattle and stop it from flowering and making seeds, and are therefore a good form of control.

Long-leafed wattle

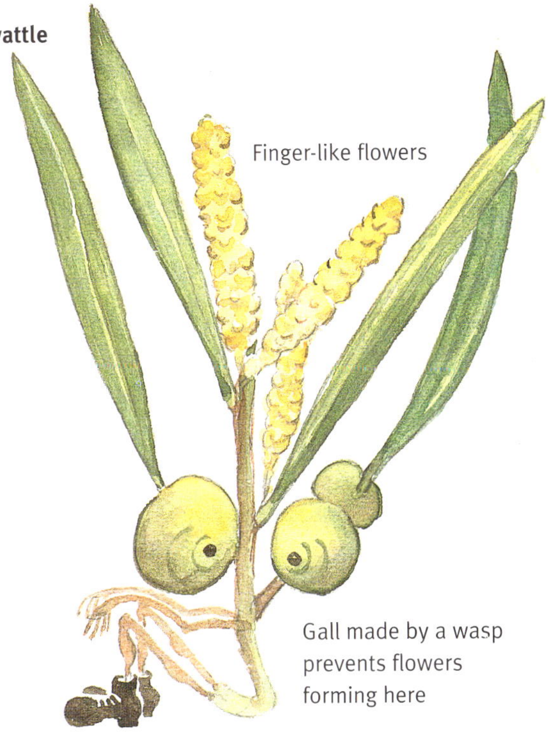

Capturing the beauty of nature

Wild flowers once grew in such numbers that you could just walk into the wilds and collect armfuls of lilies, proteas or everlastings. Now, by law, no flowers may be collected within 90 metres of a public road and permission must be sought to pick from private property. Rare or endangered plants are totally protected.

Use silver-tree leaves to make a blue crane

Identifying and recording flowers

So, what can you do if you want to record the flowers and animals that you discover? First of all, use your eyes and brain as an instant camera. Look carefully and store images of their shape, beauty and fragrance in your memory. It is helpful and fun to identify them by matching them with pictures in books (see page 61).

Capture life on film

Photography is a super way of recording what you see. For best results of flowers and insects photographers use close-up rings or a macro-lens. These give a wonderful magnified view and increase your pleasure as you compose a photo. Take time to select lovely flowers, watch the insects' behaviour and choose interesting light effects.

Keeping an eye open – when this pair of chameleons met they changed colour!

To photograph insects requires patience. The most perfect specimens may be obtained by breeding a caterpillar through to a moth or butterfly.

things to do

Decorate a candle holder: cut a circle of cardboard and stick a half ball of playdough or florist's oasis in the centre. Stand a small candle in the centre. Decorate it with silver-tree leaves, dried flowers and pods.

things to do

Grow wild herbs such as rosemary, liquorice plant, lemon-scented pelargonium, sorrel and buchu.

Paint a picture

Painting or drawing is another way of recording what you see. Remember the best way to get good results is to practise. Look carefully at the shape of a flower or animal and try to capture its character. For example, does it look delicate, papery, droopy, crisp, happy or proud? Record the leaves and fruits as well and where you found them.

Everlasting flowers with a monkey beetle.

Sea lavender or pink statice has dry papery flowers.

A wild water-wise garden

Encourage wild and indigenous plants to grow where you live. You can buy seeds and plants from Kirstenbosch Gardens. Don't mow over the bulbs that sprout each spring along roadside verges, or treat wild flowers as weeds. Indigenous plants need much less water than introduced plants. A garden with lawns, roses and hydrangeas may use six times more water than one with indigenous plants. If you grow wild flowers you will of course be able to pick them. Try and avoid using pesticides as you will kill many useful insects and birds as well.

Decorating with flowers

When arranging flowers choose colours and greenery that go well together. Proteas are heavy flowers so use a heavy vase that will not topple over. You may need to weight the vase by putting sand in the bottom of it. Arrange the greenery first and then wedge the proteas into place. Restios, everlastings, sea lavender, brunias and some of the ericas make lovely dried flowers which can be used for stylish displays with interesting logs and cones.

Pressed flowers

Pressed flowers work best with delicate or papery flowers. Large flowers may need to be cut in half or the individual petals taken off and pressed. Place you flowers flat between pieces of blotting paper in an old book or a telephone directory, put a weight on top of them and leave them for a few weeks. Stick the pressed flowers onto cards or mats and laminate them. Beautiful lampshades can be made by sandwiching pressed flowers between a sheet of iron-on vyline and a thin firm but flexible sheet of white plastic obtainable from craft shops.

things to do

Make a terrarium. Plant some seeds or a small plant in a pot and water it. Cut the top off a plastic 2-litre cooldrink bottle and use it as a transparent cover over your miniature garden. Make holes if you want to keep caterpillars or spiders.

Unusual views and lighting can turn an ordinary subject into something special.

Protecting natural areas

The Cape Flora covers such a small area of the earth's surface and yet humans have already swallowed up three-fifths of it. Although there is still a lot of natural vegetation in the mountains, introduced trees are encroaching steadily. Human activities in the valleys and on the coastal flats have all but wiped out coastal fynbos and renosterbos. Gone too are the days of picking bunches of disas and proteas from Table Mountain and looking at the water lilies in the vleis of the Salt River.

Red Data book

Threatened and endangered plants and animals are listed in Red Data Books (RDBs). This information has highlighted the plight of coastal fynbos where housing and development have used up 99 per cent of the system and several species are already extinct.

Planning for the future

It is important that we plan and work together to take responsibility for our natural heritage because everyone, whether scholar, farmer, property developer, home owner, squatter, hiker or visitor has some impact on the environment. Many organisations and nature reserves provide a life-changing environmental experience with an emphasis on awareness and first-hand discovery. The importance of environmental education has been recognised and introduced to all learning areas in the school curriculum.

things to do

Make a list of all the nature reserves within a day's journey of where you live. Try to visit them at different times of the year (see page 59).

A valuable asset

Ecotourism is becoming very popular and the Cape has wonderful opportunities to create awareness and appreciation of its natural heritage, while at the same time earning valuable income to help manage it. Property owners and farmers in the Overberg near Cape Agulhas have created a series of fynbos trails where visitors can experience the beauty of the fynbos and its animals first hand. Clanwilliam, Darling and Caledon have annual flower shows and beautiful wild flower gardens. Time spent in the veld refreshes people so they can work more efficiently.

Reitvlei, a wetland close to Cape Town, is preserved thanks to local concern and private funding.

Vital water-saving device

Water is life and fynbos is the best vegetation for ensuring a steady supply of clean water from catchment areas. Fynbos plants soak up the winter rain like a sponge but use little for their own needs. This water seeps slowly from the soil into rivers, throughout the dry summer. By contrast alien vegetation uses up vast quantities of water and allows rapid run-off that leads to soil erosion and the drying up of streams. Caring for fynbos in catchment areas provides additional water at a fraction of the cost of a new dam or desalination of sea water.

did you know?

There is a national water initiative to remove alien vegetation from water catchment areas. This programme provides work and wood for the unemployed, creates environmental awareness and can increase the water supply by 20 per cent.

The end of summer and this stream is still running at Vogelgat because the fynbos is protected from alien trees.

In a step towards creating a biosphere reserve, 18 private properties next to the Cederberg Wilderness Area will soon be private nature reserves.

Biosphere reserves

A biosphere reserve is a unique reserve catering for people and nature. The reserve is zoned and may include a strictly conserved area surrounded by a buffer zone where environmental principles are practised by farmers and property owners, and recreational facilities are made available. This affords control over ecotourism and increases the value of the area. Factories and settlements bordering on a reserve also need to be environmentally friendly and not cause land, air, water or noise pollution.

did you know?

Property owners in the Hermanus area are working together to combat alien vegetation around the lagoon and in the mountains. As an incentive, funds have been made available to cover half of their costs.

Conservation areas in the Cape Floral Kingdom

De Hoop, a reserve east of Cape Agulhas, has a wonderful range of habitats including a marine haven, dune fields, a wetland, bat caves and fynbos. Mountain zebras, bontebok, vultures, blue cranes, wading birds, snakes and tortoises can be seen there.

Fortunately there are many protected areas in the Cape Floral Kingdom but most of them are in the mountains. Recently new parks have been proclaimed to include other vulnerable habitats. The Cape Peninsula National Park protects both the mountain chain and stretches of coast as well. The West Coast National Park includes the valuable wetlands of Langebaan Lagoon, while Tsitsikamma National Park is a marvellous marine and forest reserve.

A new approach

In recent years a wave of environmental awareness and ecotourism has swept the world. In South Africa there has been a change of emphasis so that management includes both natural and man-made environments, where people and wildlife both have a right to exist. There is also a change from top down management by government to one involving local communities in decision making. This encourages co-operation and ownership with a share in the profits from conservation.

things to do

Do you know of natural areas that should be protected? Consider contacting local government authorities, nature conservation organisations, farm owners or private individuals to make them aware of these potential reserve areas. Challenge property developers to keep areas free for natural fynbos and not convert it all to houses, sports fields or grassy park land.

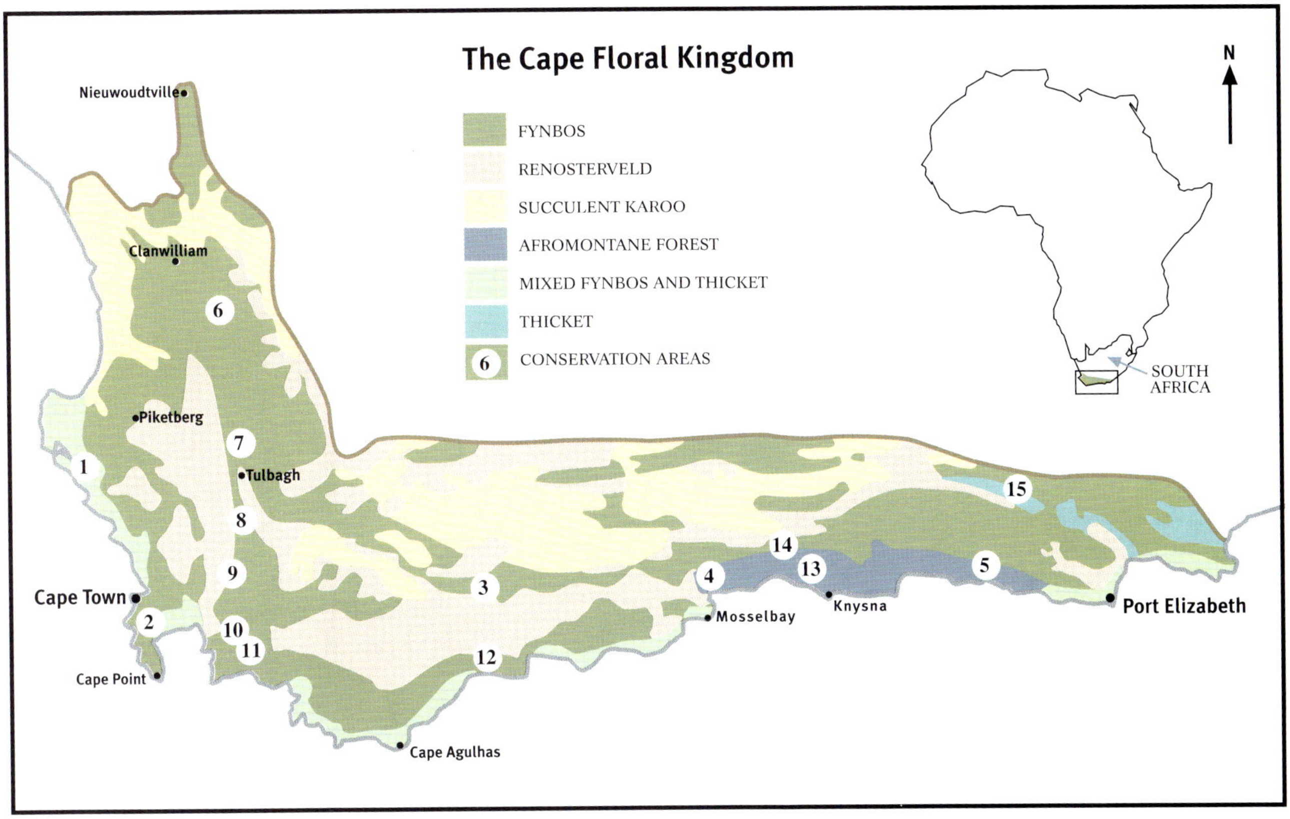

Some popular parks and reserves

National Parks

Reservations for accommodation
South African National Parks
Cape Town – PO Box 7400, Roggebaai 8021
Tel (021) 222810/6
Fax (021) 24 6211

Pretoria – PO Box 787, Pretoria 0001
Tel (012) 343 1991
Fax (021) 343 0905
E mail: reservations@parks-sa.co.za

(1) West Coast National Park at Langebaan Lagoon and Postberg Nature Reserve
Tel (02287) 22144/5
Fax (02287) 22607

(2) Cape Peninsula National Park at Cape Town

(3) Bontebok National Park at Swellendam
Tel (0291) 42735
Fax (0291) 42646

(4) Wilderness National Park (Garden Route) near George
Tel (0441) 877 1197
Fax (0441) 877 0111

(5) Tsitsikamma National Park (Garden Route) Storms River Mouth and Nature's Valley
Tel (042) 541 1607
Fax (042) 541 1629

Cape Nature Conservation and Eastern Cape Nature Conservation Reserves

(6) Cederberg Wilderness Area Citrusdal and Clanwillian P Bag x1 Citrusdal 7340
Tel (027) 482 2403
Fax (027) 482 2406

(7) Groot Winterhoek Wilderness Area near Tulbagh P O Box 26 Porterville 6810
Tel (02623) 2900
Fax (02623) 2913

(8) Limietberg Nature Reserve Du Toits Kloof and Bains Kloof and Boland Hiking Trail

(9) Jonkershoek Nature Reserve (Boland Hiking Trail) P Bag x1 Uniedal 7612
Tel (021) 889 1560

(10) Hottentots Holland Nature Reserve
P Bag x27 Elgin 7180
Tel (0225) 4826
Fax (0225) 4457

(11) Kogelberg Nature Reserve
P Bag x1 Kleinmond 7195
Tel & Fax (028) 272 8425

(12) De Hoop Nature Reserve and Potberg Environmental Education Centre
P Bag X16 Bredasdorp 7280
Tel (028) 542 1126
Fax (028) 542 1897

(13) Goukamma Nature Reserve between Knysna and Sedgefield P O Box 331 Knysna 6570
Tel & Fax (0445) 83 0042

(14) Outeniqua Nature Reserve and Hiking Trail
P Bag X 6517 George 6530
Tel (044) 870 8323
Fax (044) 870 7138

(15) Baviaanskloof and Formosa State Forests inland from Jeffries Bay P Bag 203 Willowmore 6680

Notes to teachers

Active learning

discuss
discover
think
act

Explore the Cape Flora and Curriculum 2005

Environmental education themes

Explore the Cape Flora is a dynamic book designed to develop life skills and increase an awareness and appreciation for the Cape Floral Kingdom. Each spread is a theme in itself. Important information and recent scientific findings are given to provide a framework for learners' self-discovery.

Outcomes-based education: developing life skills

Readers are encouraged to discover first-hand the wonderful variety of plants and animals and to watch how they interact. Practical 'things to do' are suggested to challenge learners to experiment and find out by themselves or in groups and so expand on the information given.

This book has already been used in schools and proved its worth in increasing general knowledge and developing skills in observation, critical thinking and practical application. Learners are encouraged to have responsible attitudes towards maintaining a healthy and sustainable environment. They will become aware of the value of the Cape Flora for creating jobs and wealth and the importance of conserving its incredible biodiversity while being sensitive to cultural issues. The book provides a variety of activities suitable for a cross-curricular approach and could enhance all learning areas of the Curriculum 2005, if used with imagination. Many of the critical outcomes of the school curriculum can be achieved by using these themes.

Assessment

Continual assessment can be achieved using project work, oral presentation, group discussions and problem-solving exercises.

Some useful references

Cowling, R. & Richardson, D. 1995, *Fynbos: South Africa's unique Floral Kingdom* Fernwood Press, Vlaeberg, Cape Town

Fraser, M. & McMahon, L. 1994, *Between Two Shores* David Philip, Cape Town

Hilton-Taylor, C. 1996, *Red Data list of South African plants* National Botanical Institute

Levy, J. 1989, *The Complete Guide to Walks and Trails in Southern Africa* Struik, Cape Town

McMahon, L. & Fraser, M. 1988, *A Fynbos Year* David Philip, Cape Town

Palmer, E. *The South African Herbal* Tafelberg, Cape Town

Paterson-Jones, C. 1991, *Table Mountain Walks* Struik, Cape Town

Roberts, M. 1990, *Indigenous Healing Plants* Southern Book Publishers

Rourke, J. P. 1980, *The Proteas of Southern Africa* Purnell, CapeTown

Schumann, D. & Kirsten, G. 1992, *Ericas of South Africa* Fernwood Press, Cape Town

Stirton, C. H. (ed), 1987, *Plant invaders: Beautiful but dangerous* Department of Nature and Environmental Conservation of the CPA, Cape Town

Van der Walt, J. J. 1977, *Pelargoniums of South Africa 1, 2, 3* Juta, Cape Town

Van Wyk, B., van Oudtshoorn, B. & Gericke, N. 1997, *Medicinal Plants of South Africa* Briza, Pretoria

South African Wild Flower Guides, Botanical Society of South Africa

1 Namaqualand and Clanwilliam 1988
2 Outeniqua Tsitsikamma and Eastern Little Karroo 1982
3 Cape Peninsula 1983
5 Hottentots Holland to Hermanus 1985
6 Karoo 1994
7 West coast 1994
8 Niewoudtville 1997

Popular journals

Africa: Environment and Wildlife, P Borchert (ed) P O Box 44223, Claremont 7735, CapeTown

Geological Society of South Africa Pamphlets, P O Box 572, Bellville 7535

Veld and Flora, The Botanical Society, P Bag X10, Newlands 7725

African Wildlife, Wildlife and Environment Society of South Africa, P O Box 44189, Linden 2104

Some useful contacts

Many of these organisations produce excellent magazines or teaching aids

Botanical Society of South Africa
Kirstenbosch, Claremont 7735
Tel (021) 797 2090 (Branches nationwide)

Cape Nature Conservation
P Bag X9086, Cape Town 8000
Tel (021) 483 4227

EnviroTeach
PO Box 7870, Johannesburg 2000
Tel (011) 835 2221

Mountain Club of South Africa
97 Hatfield Street, CapeTown 8001

National Botanical Institute (includes National Botanical Gardens)
at Kirstenbosch National Botanical Garden
P Bag X7, Claremont 7735
Tel (021) 762 1166

Share-Net and Environmental Education Association of Southern Africa (EEASA)
PO Box 394, Howick 3290
Tel (0332) 305 721

Trees for Africa
PO Box 2035, Gallo Manor 2052
Tel (011) 803 9750

University of Cape Town
Rondebosch 7700

Botany and Bolus Herbarium
Tel (021) 650 4037 Fax (021) 650 4041

Institute for Plant Conservation
Tel (021) 650 2440 Fax (021) 650 4046

Ornithology
Tel (021) 650 3297 Fax (021) 650 3295

Zoology
Tel (021) 650 3604 Fax (021) 650 3301

University of Port Elizabeth
Botany
Tel (041) 504 2111

University of Stellenbosch
Botany
Tel (021) 808 3054

University of the Western Cape
P Bag X17, Bellville 7535
Botany and Environmental Education and Resources Unit
Tel (021) 959 2498 Fax (021) 959 2266

Wildlife and Environmental Society of South Africa (WESSA)
Head Office PO Box 394, Howick 3290
Tel (0332) 30391 (Branches nationwide)

Eastern Province Region
2b Lawrence Street, Central Hill, Port Elizabeth 6001
Tel (041) 559606 Fax (041) 563228

Southern Cape Region
c/o Pledge Nature Reserve, Bond Street, Knysna 6570
Tel/Fax (0445) 810237

Western Cape Region
PO Box 30145, Tokai 7966
The Sanctuary, off Pollsmoor Road, Kirstenhof 7945
Tel (021) 701 1397/8 Fax (021) 701 1399

World Wide Fund for Nature in South Africa (WWF – SA)
PO Box 456 Stellenbosch 7599
Tel (021) 887 2801 Fax (021) 887 9517

Keywords
for *Explore the Cape Flora*

species ecology anther eyrie larva

adaptation a modification of plants or animals which enables them to be better able to survive and reproduce

alien plant a plant introduced from another country

anther the male part of the flower which produces pollen

artificial respiration restarting breathing after it has stopped, for example, by mouth-to-mouth breathing

biodiversity the wide variety of plant and animal species in their natural environment

bract a single specialised leaf on a flower stalk

bulb a modified stem enclosed in fleshy leaves that contain food reserves. An organ of vegetative reproduction

corm swollen, underground stem base that stores food and produces new plants from its buds. An organ of vegetative reproduction

caffeine a chemical found in coffee and tea that acts as a stimulant

camouflaged blending in with the colours and shapes of the natural surroundings and so being difficult to see

capsule a dry fruit that releases its seeds by opening in various ways

catchment area the area of land draining into a river or reservoir

condense when a gas changes into a liquid

conservation the protection, preservation and management of natural resources and the environment

cotyledon a specialised leaf, inside the seed, which stores starch and provides energy for germination; it sometimes forms the first leaf after germination

deciduous plants which lose their leaves at certain seasons e.g. autumn

desalination removing salt from sea water so that it can be used for drinking or irrigation

dormant when a plant or an animal is alive but in a resting state

ecology the study of the relationships between living organisms and their environment

endemic a plant or an animal which is confined to a given region

evergreen plants that have leaves throughout the year

evaporate when a liquid changes into a gas

extinct a species of plant or animal which has died out

eyrie the nest of a bird of prey, for example, an eagle, usually built in a high, inaccessible place, such as a rocky ledge

fertilisation the fusing of the nucleus of the male gamete with the nucleus of the female gamete to produce a zygote

fertiliser a substance which is added to the soil to increase the growth of plants, such as manure or a mixture of chemicals

fluorescent a substance which gives out light

gamete – reproductive cell usually differentiated into male (sperm in mammals) and female (ovum) which fuse during fertilisation

geophyte plant that spends part of the year underground as a swollen bulb or corms and survives the dry summer

germinate when a seed starts to grow and produces roots and shoots

habitat the place where a plant or an animal lives

hormone (growth) an organic substance produced in minute quantities that stimulates growth in plants

hypothesis an idea to explain a particular phenomenon or group of facts

indigenous naturally occurring in an area

KhoiKhoi (or KhoeKhoe) early African herders

KhoiSan hunter-gatherers and herders

kloof a mountain pass or gorge

larva a pre-adult stage in the life cycle of some animals which hatch from an egg and change into an adult. The larva is different from the adult, e.g. a caterpillar of a butterfly and a tadpole of a frog habitat stamens fertiliser pest corm nectar pollen sap

mineral salt a chemical substance, such as calcium nitrate, needed by plants for healthy growth

national park an area of environmental or scenic importance, designated by the government for public use. In South Africa national parks are managed by South African National Parks

nature reserve an area of land that is protected and managed to preserve a particular habitat and the plants and animals that live there. In South Africa nature reserves are under local, private or provincial management

nectar sugary liquid produced by flowers that is collected by bees and other insects

nocturnal an animal that is active at night; a plant that has flowers which open at night and close during the day

nodules swellings on the roots of certain plants of the pea and bean family (legumes) that contain nitrogen-fixing bacteria. By their activity soil is enriched in nitrogen which is essential for plant growth.

parasite a plant or an animal that lives in or on another, described as the host, and absorbs food from the host

pest a troublesome or destructive plant or animal

photosynthesis the making of sugars and starches by a green plant from carbon dioxide and water, using energy from sunlight

pollen the fine powder produced by the male part of the flower, containing the male sex cells

pollination the transfer of pollen from the anther (the male part of a flower) to the stigma (the female part of a flower)

poultice a moist pad that contains substances used to treat an inflamed area of skin

predator a carnivorous animal (or, rarely, a plant) that eats animals, known as prey

quagga a subspecies of the plains zebra that has a sandy-brown colour with zebra-like stripes on the head and shoulders

San African people who lived a life based on hunting and gathering food

sanctuary a place protected by law where plants and animals can live without being disturbed

sap the solution of water and mineral salts and food that circulates in a plant

sense organ a specialised part of an animal, such as the eye, that receives stimuli from the surroundings and transmits them to the brain

species members of a group of animals or plants with common characteristics that can breed with each other; the smallest unit of classification. Each species has two names, the first denotes the genus to which it belongs (along with other related species) and the second, the specific name which is unique to that species, e.g. *Erica ovina*

spore a part of a plant that can develop into a new plant, usually microscopic, the reproductive unit of algae, fungi, mosses and ferns of simple plants, e.g. protozoa

stamens male part of the flower consisting of anther and filament (stalk)

stigma female part of the flower which receives the pollen

stoma (stomata pl.) tiny pore surrounded by a pair of guard cells in the surface layer of a leaf that allows air to enter and leave the leaf

succulents plants which store water in thick fleshy stems or leaves

symbiosis a close relationship between two organisms that is of benefit to both

terrarium a container for keeping plants or small animals with a transparent cover

tourniquet a bandage tied tightly around an arm or a leg to prevent blood flow in an artery or a vein and to control bleeding

tuber swollen underground root or stem that contains food reserves

ultraviolet light part of the electromagnetic spectrum that has short wavelengths, just beyond the violet end of the visible spectrum

variation differences between individual plants and animals of the same species

venom the poisonous fluid secreted by animals such as snakes and scorpions, usually transmitted by a sting or bite

Index